Reweaving the Sacred

Reweaving the Sacred

A Practical Guide to
Change and Growth for
Challenged Congregations

CAROL J. GALLAGHER

CHURCH PUBLISHING
an imprint of
Church Publishing Incorporated, New York

Library of Congress Cataloging-in-Publication Data

Gallagher, Carol.
　　Reweaving the sacred : a practical guide to change and growth
for challenged congregations / Carol J. Gallagher.
　　　　p.　　　cm.
　　ISBN 978-0-89869-588-5 (pbk.)
　　1. Church renewal.　2. Church growth.　3. Change—Religious
aspects—Christianity. I. Title.
BV600.3.G34　　2008
253—dc22

　　　　　　　　　　　　　　　　　　　　　　　2008005692

Cover by Brenda Klinger
Interior by Beth Oberholtzer Design

Church Publishing Incorporated
445 Fifth Avenue
New York NY 10016
www.churchpublishing.org

5　4　3　2　1

This book is dedicated to my husband, Mark,
who is most brilliant and who gives love,
encouragement, laughter, and light to my every day;
to our beautiful and brilliant daughters,
Emily, Ariel, and Phoebe who cover me with
laughter and enthusiasm; and to my Mom and Dad,
who taught me to pray and rejoice in who
I am as a Cherokee and a child of God;
I couldn't have done any of this without you.

Wa-do (Thank-you).

Contents

CHAPTER ONE

Discovering Gifts
Relationship and Identity

*(Can be used during the seasons
of Christmas and Epiphany)*

Can you imagine a bright, sunny Sunday morning and that wonderful moment when a family is gathered at the front of the church, surrounded by godparents, neighbors, friends, and well wishers, to have their child baptized? The hopes and dreams of this family, along with those of the entire gathered community, are centered on the one little person, possibly dressed in some gossamer, frilly outfit, handed down, from generation to generation. The water is poured over the child's head, and then holy oil is pressed on the child's forehead. "You are marked as Christ's own forever!" a cheery priest proclaims and the entire gathering is alive with applause, music, and congratulations. This is a joyful moment in the life of every church. It can be a time of great welcome, deepening of relationships, and expanding of our common identity. Too often it is an isolated occasion without much connection.

The same group of people, who pledged to help raise this child in the faith and in community, might well have to struggle to understand the faith they have received and may never truly understand how to share their faith journey. They may never understand Christ's mission in that particular community. They may feel unequipped to do so. The parents may never have knowledge of God's unique call to them or their family within that community. The parents themselves might feel inadequate to the task. We are called to be Christ's own forever, to possess a unique identity in, and relationship to Jesus Christ, and yet we often feel unable to tell our story as it relates to the Jesus story. This dilemma is particularly true among congregations that are small or isolated; congregations that may have declined due to economic hardships; churches founded to respond to specific racial or cultural situations in very different times. The true story of the people, of the community, might never be heard by this child or by the child's family. Many church communities are fractured by the changes they have undergone and have become discouraged, feeling that their best days of ministry are behind them.

This book is for the leadership of any congregation that has experienced the fracturing and hardships that make it very difficult to envision growth and vitality for their church. This book is for anyone struggling with how to respond to God's call in their special community—and for those who are wrestling to find themselves and their community in the larger story of the Christian faith. My goal is to remind communities that God has called each of us into existence and called us for an incredible purpose. This book is meant to encourage individuals and congregations to discover what that purpose is within their particular place and community. It is designed to invite growth through discovering and using the gifts each community has been given by God. Whether, as a community, you are small or isolated, different or distressed, there is more that God would have you do, right where you are planted. You have a story to tell and there are people desperate to be touched and welcomed to that unique place where you find yourselves.

Unique

First, let me explain what I mean by a unique congregation or community. As a bishop in the Episcopal Church, I have had the joy of being in many, many churches across the dioceses I have served. I was once in a very small, rural congregation for an evening meeting. This was a congregation that was often described by outsiders and diocesan leaders as one of our "dying parishes." When I arrived, rain was coming down in torrents. The senior warden wanted me to see the sanctuary of the church before we moved to the meeting. I wasn't sure why he was so insistent, but I reluctantly went along with him, in the rain, across the grass lawn from the little building that served as a parish hall to the one-story wooden structure, barely visible from the road. He took me inside to a church that could seat about seventy people at full capacity. And then he slowly walked me around the church, touching each and every pew and pointing out pulpit and lectern, the crosses and the windows. He told me the name of every person who had carved each pew, and their relationship to a present member of the congregation. For him, these were not objects or things, but rather the symbols of a living faith passed on from a previous generation. In the pews lived the stories of freed field slaves, of women, men, and children, their sorrows and joys and the faith that he had inherited from them all. In the simple objects of that humble space, great deeds of faithfulness and God's promise and commitment were made very real. His stories wove the bigger story of our faith in Christ.

This tiny congregation, which might seem dreary or doomed to outsiders, was alive and vibrant with ministry and outreach. Despite their limited numbers, the people of the congregation provided opportunities and training for many children in their community and have set up a computer lab, teaching children and adults how to use the internet and other online resources. All of the computers were rescued from businesses that were upgrading their technology. They take children and young

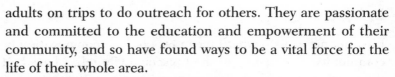

adults on trips to do outreach for others. They are passionate and committed to the education and empowerment of their community, and so have found ways to be a vital force for the life of their whole area.

Every congregation, every building, every community has a unique and often challenging life. Every congregation is unique, and people have come there because they have found solace, compassion, and a home in Jesus among the people gathered. Like the little congregation I just described, many small churches (whether rural or urban) might seem troubled or even dying to outsiders. But to those who have been ministered to, or those who have found a home among those who were once strangers, that church is at the heart of their lives and their hopes for the future. It is our human struggle and our faith in Christ all woven together in the mystery of God's love and presence with us.

This book, I hope, will provide encouragement and suggest some ways forward to growth, using the unique symbols, stories, and strength that are the people of God in your unique place. It will help tell the story of the faith that has been inherited and help find ways to use that strength to serve a present, reconfigured community.

Relationship

Throughout this book, I will be emphasizing the importance of *relationship*. As a Native American woman (Cherokee), I was raised to understand that I was related to a very large human family and an even larger created cosmos. Native people speak of all of our relations to describe not only the human family, but the four-legged and other creatures who share this fragile earth with us. My elders taught me that I was never alone. I learned that every morning I had more to care for than just myself. Every morning and every evening, I was to consider all that was around me and all those with whom I shared the day. Every day I was to consider my responsibility for those around me—that day and every day. As tribal people, we are constantly concerned that our individual work and actions will bring honor to our people. If we are not careful, we can dishonor our people by being selfish and acting in a disrespectful way. We believe that we are called to take care of the welfare, health, and survival of all people in our midst, even those we might consider our enemy. What I learned from an early age was that relationships were more important than programs or policies, and that relationships were more important than theologies and politics. I was taught that all living creatures take precedence over transactions, success, and business affairs. Who we are and how we are for others was to be the critical concern for any faithful person.

Relationships are the building blocks of every congregation and community. Some of us are fortunate enough to come into a particular congregation because we were born into a family that was part of a given community. I was born, the fourth of five children, to a Presbyterian minister and his Cherokee wife. Both of my parents were intimately involved in the church, and when I was a very small child I had the misguided notion that my Daddy owned the church where he served. I did not have to think about my relationships in this community because my role was clear and the expectations were defined for me.

Some people do not have the opportunity to have a natural relationship with a single church or community. Many Americans have been brought up in very complex families where their relationship to a community of faith was only in the form of a battleground between families. Others have had little or no exposure to faith communities and have no story or experience with people in these places. I was given a relationship with an entire group of people, because of who my parents were and what they did. Others have had to feel their way around in the dark and find their way into communities that seem to give no clue as to who is who and what they are doing there. There are no roadmaps of the relationships in a given church, and people often walk away because they can find no way to connect their story to the stories of others. They are looking for how they can relate to others, and how God fits into their life story.

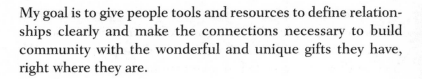

My goal is to give people tools and resources to define relationships clearly and make the connections necessary to build community with the wonderful and unique gifts they have, right where they are.

Centrality of Story

I will use a variety of stories to illustrate situations and experiences that I have had in my own faith journey (as both a clergy and lay person) that are common to most people who worship in a church community. But there is much more to the story than mere illustration. For Native people, stories have power to illuminate and change the course of history. Stories both define and redefine us, as we seek God's wisdom in the midst of the story. The biblical narrative unfolds the power of God's love for humanity in its complex and rich diversity throughout history. We see ourselves in the lives of those who have come before, as we struggle with the parables of Jesus, just as his disciples did. Stories are more than picture books for learning, but can generate a true spiritual movement and an insight not gained by words and instruction alone. Narrative reasoning, the logic of wrapping oneself in the story in order to come out the other side with a new notion of truth, might be challenging for some who are steeped in normative Western European thought. I invite you to dive into the idea of learning through story and you will discover the world around your congregation through the *collective story*, which will reveal the collected wisdom of the community and therefore the heart of God in your midst.

The story is central to the work of this book, as you will be, over and over again, asked to hear and retell the story of your common life as a church family and a broader community. I firmly believe that the way forward for any struggling congregation will be found in the story that is revealed and which will point to the future—to where God is calling you, as a group, to go. Many of us give in to the notion of decline and collapse, because we haven't been encouraged or enlightened by a story that lifts our hearts and minds and that invites us to join others in faith and service. Many of us have lost sight of why we came to this church in the first place. If you gain nothing more than learning anew to delight in the community God has given you, then you will still have gained a future of hope and possibility. Your story and the story of your people, your community, your surroundings is essential to the life of the church. Your story is embedded in God's story—the story that tells us that God so loved the world (and each and every one of us) that he gave us his only Son. God gave up a child that we might all be part of God's story, of God's family. So tell your stories, knowing God is in the midst of these stories and in the hearts and minds of the people around you.

I learned this lesson quite vividly when I was a relatively new bishop. My visitation schedule took me to a rural parish in the western part of the diocese. The visit time was set for two o'clock in the afternoon, and I was coming there from another church. This small parish always had an afternoon service, so it was convenient for me to go from one town to the other. When I arrived, only the senior warden and one other person was there. Often, the senior warden explained, they had to wait for folks who were getting off their morning jobs—and who might also need to pick a up a family member on the way—before they could start their service. He suggested that he often began with a Bible study or church school lesson, so I followed his advice.

Since it was Advent, and across the church parishes were struggling with stewardship campaigns, I talked with them a bit about stewardship. I pulled a penny out of my pocket and we talked about what a penny could buy. "Not much, today," one person said, and we went on to talk about what a penny had bought when they were children. At this point, a group of about eight people had gathered, all of them well over 70. They began to tell me about their lives as children, the challenges they had just trying to make ends meet, and their great pride in their church. "This is where we all got together!" someone commented. And then they told about the people and labor that went into creating the church building. When I asked about when the church was built, everyone looked at the oldest woman there. She was regal in her dress and bearing and took her time answering my question. "Well," she finally said, "my cousin hadn't moved to Chicago yet and she moved to Chicago in 1920, so it must be sometime right before that." She told of having to wait, as a small child, until her mother and father got done with their work, feeding and cleaning up after the Sunday meal for their white employer, who owned the largest farm in the area. "This church has always been in the afternoon, since I can remember," she told me, "and we often went on singing and praising God well into the evening!"

I went on to pull out a sandwich bag filled with pennies and we talked about what a bunch of pennies could do together. We laughed about the fact that I had raided my daughter's piggy bank to bring all these pennies, and then we talked about the little we might each contribute, but how together, we could grow something larger. Again, the oldest woman there talked about how little they had as children, and yet how great the things they had done together had been. "We had a choir that you would not have believed," she said, "and we sang across the county and even for the governor." They told some stories of the past, but also of the ministries that were ongoing in their community. When several more families had gathered, the senior warden suggested, quite subtly, that it was time to begin the service. We sang and prayed and had Communion together. Afterward, we crowded into the small vestibule and shared wonderful food and more stories. I felt rich and full when our visit was done.

As I headed out the door, the warden handed me an envelope with the church's cash contribution for the bishop's discretionary fund. In a little brown envelope, weary and crumpled with age, were 14 dollars. Words from Mark's gospel immediately came to mind. "Truly I tell you, this poor widow has put in more than all those who are contributing to the treasury. For all of them have contributed out of their abundance; but she out of her poverty has put in everything she had, all she had to live on." I knew I was in the presence of those who knew the heart and truth of Christ, and their story became for me a witness to God's abundant love in the midst of our lives. Theirs was the largest and most generous contribution my discretionary fund received.

Hearing their story and talking to them that day, the importance of story became clear. The real impact of the gospel is in the lives of the people. No one can guess what the story of your church community is, and if they guess, they will probably guess wrong. It takes a whole group of people sharing their experiences for the full story to come to light, with depth, color, and the vibrancy of a living tradition—your tradition, your story. The power of story can be seen as the light of the gospel story permeating and saturating the living mission of your congregation.

Identity

Finally, it is important to understand the crucial role that a clear and articulated identity plays in the ability of a faith community to welcome and include people who were once strangers. All communities have particular identities. When my husband and I were first married, we struggled with finding a church home, where we would go, and how we honor both of our family spiritual traditions. Both of us had been raised in Christian homes. I was raised as a "preacher's kid" in the Presbyterian Church and he was raised in a devout Roman Catholic family. We tried for a time to go to church together, alternating his communion and mine, changing about every month, or sometimes every new season. The one thing we knew for sure is that we wanted to worship together. It didn't take us long to learn that worship meant something different to each of us. Our identities had been formed in particular ways by our parents and our churches. Neither tradition was a home for the both of us. Many couples struggle with this loss of faith identity before and after marriage or union. Some choose to skip participating in a church or faith community entirely because the situation proves to be too hard to sort out.

Many couples struggle, as we did, because with marriage or union their individual identities have changed. We were no longer completely who we used to be. By committing one's life to another, our self-concepts are stretched out beyond where they used to be. Committed relationships call us to see ourselves, and each other, with new eyes in the midst of different people who want to help define us. Long-term relationships are just one way our self-understanding changes. Geographic moves, loss, childbirth, new employment (or loss of employment) can change our identities. We are not what we used to be and we are not yet what we shall become. This transitory state is often the point at which people come seeking a faith home.

Some people, when seeking a faith home, fall back on what their parents did. Some keep their lives of faith separate from their families and other relationships. Many of us cannot return to our inherited traditions because it may not be an option. We choose to struggle with the ambiguity of our lives and seek a community in which we can belong. What we knew before no longer has the taste and welcome of home. All people, in times of transition, seek places and people who can help them reform their concept of self. A clear identity is important to healthy human beings. Without it we cannot face the challenges of daily life without great risk. Much of what local faith communities can do for people, and what most people are seeking, is a place where they are recognized for who they are, and where they are able to grow and develop with a sense of safety and security.

My Cherokee grandfather wrote this about his own personal identity when, as children, we asked him to tell us the story of his life. "It is about time I told you that I am a Cherokee Indian named S-onet-nee Oo-dahl-uh-nunh-sti, the one you know as Gramps, and father of your mother, Betty. I was born on the banks of the Bear Creek in a double log cabin at the town of Tahlequah ['two is enough']), the capital of the Cherokee nation. Tahlequah got its name, it is said, because when the Cherokees arrived at this well-watered and timbered place, the tribe stopped, sent out three parties in three directions to ride for days to find the best place for the tribe to settle down. A month went by and only two of the parties had returned. The third party was never heard from again. No trace. They possibly came into contact with some western band on the prowl and were wiped out. But the leader of the Cherokees, with two exploring parties back, said, 'two is enough.' They had found no place as fine as where they were right there."

My grandfather, telling the story of his origins and his identity, also tells the story of his people, and in his telling their identities are interwoven. Our identities, both as individuals and as members of a church community, are intertwined with the identities of the communities where we live and of the people with whom we share our lives. We are also formed and identified by our racial and ethnic heritages and by the language and traditions we have been brought up to embrace as our own. All of a people's stories weave a strong thread that is also interlaced with the gospel story, for those of us who know their identity within the life of our community church. As Christians, the fabric that we share within our own tradition becomes part of our living identity in Christ.

When Mark and I married in Relay, Maryland, in 1975, my father and a Roman Catholic priest from Mark's tradition officiated together at our wedding. As a new couple, we needed to find a church home where we could worship together and bring our children up to be followers of Christ. We needed a community that would welcome our diversity and not try to "reform" or change us, but would take us as we were. We have always been artistic, creative types, fascinated with the multitude of expressions that constitute God's love in the world. On top of that, since I was brought up by a fairly traditional Cherokee mother, I was steeped in traditional Native beliefs and behaviors and was challenged to find a place where my Native roots were not considered outside the pale (literally). Many Native people, myself included, have a complex relationship with the church, as many of our families have been Christians for generations but the church did not take kindly to our traditions and ways, at least in the past. And so there is hesitancy to enter a church community that might unintentionally reject a person simply because of who they are. Together, my husband and I sought an authentic expression of community, one that would welcome and include a mixed race, creative couple and their children.

In 1982, after years of going back and forth between communions, a friend invited us to the Episcopal Church, specifically to St. John's Church, Mount Washington. He told us about this Episcopal parish, which was filled with all sorts of what he described as creative and artistic folks. He thought we might find it a place where we could become part of the community and lend our gifts to their efforts. Neither of us had attended an Episcopal church before on a Sunday, although we had been to several Episcopal weddings. We went our first Sunday—and never looked back. There were young families and elders there and everyone seemed to take an interest in us. We had found a home.

The Episcopal Church, in its local manifestation in the Diocese of Maryland and through St. John's, taught me that the church could be a place of welcome and inclusion. I learned that challenging questions, diverse theologies, and biblical interpretations could be celebrated. It was from this place that I was molded as a Christian, deepened in faith, and encouraged to seek Christ in every aspect of my life. I was inspired to answer God's call to explore ordained ministry from this place. They trusted a young, headstrong woman with small, fierce daughters, loving and encouraging Mark and me every step of the way. My firm foundation of faith was formed in a rich soil of trust and inclusion, a garden where the people of God saw hope and possibility in every human being and in every relationship.

The faith community (parish and diocese), in its diversity of leaders, women and men, lay and ordained, journeyed with me as I explored this call. They took risks in following Christ. The faith community at St. John's was so firm in its own identity that the people were able to reach out with open arms and to express clearly their welcome and need of us. It was from that one small invitation that a lifelong relationship began and it was from that parish that I was sponsored for ordained ministry. They helped me to know who I was, and who God was calling me to be. They were secure enough in their identity to allow us to grow secure in our own identities. Knowing who you are as a community is essential for welcoming and reaching out to others. My hope is that this book can be an encouragement for all those places that think they have nothing to offer, and that it can help clergy and communities to grow strong in who they are, where they are, and where God is calling them.

It can also be the case that a rich and powerful identity can be lost or destroyed, usually unintentionally, but that loss can make everyone, whether directly connected or distantly related, feel less accepted and even set aside. The goal of this book is to point out ways in which we can enrich one another and nurture our gifts; but all too often, the church has overlooked those gifts and we are all less because of that shortsightedness. Diocesan leadership may look from outside and see what they might call "a dying congregation." All too often, no one takes the time to learn the true story of the people, to see their gifts and their hope for the future. All too often, doors are closed for lack of a story that can project a future of faith and hope.

I want to share with you this example, which is one of many of my experience as a priest and bishop in the Episcopal Church. Several years ago, I was visiting a suburban parish on the edge of a large and depressed city. This parish was founded nearly 100 years ago by a group of African American families that had felt unwelcome and excluded in their town's predominantly white parishes. These families had been Episcopalians for generations, and despite the lip service of the clergy and people in these predominantly white congregations, the black families realized that their leadership and gifts were not welcome in these places. Although legal segregation was no longer in effect, segregation was still the order of the day. They had spent years sitting in the balcony, looking down into a congregation that could not understand or welcome their stories and experiences. They felt talked about, and invited, but not really wanted or understood. They had very little money with which to purchase a building, but were fortunate enough to find an old armory building that was not in use, which the government was willing to sell to them at a very reasonable price.

When I visited with them in early June, the world outside was alive with color and bright blue skies. The severe squat building stood in contrast to the bright green of the trees and the yellows and blues of the flowers that were planted all around. When I entered the very non-descript, non-church-like structure, my eyes were immediately drawn to the ornate and colorful ceiling. On the ceiling were painted, in a glorious Victorian style, many biblical scenes with the stories of the scripture seemingly come to life. I was struck dumb by the beauty and power of the artwork, but even more by the symbolism. Here we were, about to worship together, in a building that had once been used to stockpile weapons and train soldiers. Here I was, among people who had suffered rejection and injustice, but were claiming and proclaiming God's transforming love, despite it all. Now, this armory had been transformed into a holy and sacred place where God's peace and love for every creature was preached and demonstrated. The words from Isaiah 2 came flooding to mind. "For out of Zion shall go forth instruction, and the word of the Lord from Jerusalem. He shall judge between the nations, and shall arbitrate for many peoples; they shall beat their swords into plowshares, and their spears into pruning hook; nation shall not lift up sword against nation, neither shall they learn war any more. O house of Jacob, come, let us walk in the light of the Lord!" Here was a congregation of people, heirs of the rejection of their neighbors, who were still declaring their hope in God, and graphically depicting their belief that God was in their midst, despite the warring of nations and people. I truly believed that this was an important place for the whole diocese and church to see and understand.

Unfortunately, within a year's time, due to very profound financial circumstances and the lack of human resources, this parish was forced to close, and their remnant membership has had to join in with another congregation. I don't want to suggest that there was anyone in leadership that did anything wrong in these circumstances. My sadness is with the loss of a great history and a great icon of hope for God's peace among people. Was there something else that might have been done, if this great legacy and gift had been seen for what it was? A gift and legacy for more than just the few gathered, but for the extended community, which had suffered through many financial and political hardships? If time and resources had come to bear in these circumstances, could a new vision for mission and ministry have been dreamed, and implemented, for these people and their community? If someone had listened to their story, if there had been a way to reach out and hear God's call in their midst, could this richness have been saved to help others gain in faith and hope? Our task in this book is to find ways to help every congregation that wishes to continue and grow in the service of Christ and their fellow human beings to find a future.

Identifying Gifts

There will be exercises or activities at the end of each chapter of this book that can help identify gifts, stimulate learning, and encourage congregational growth. One of the essential elements of this work is listening to God, which is not a one time or seasonal exercise. The best way to listen to God is through reading and studying the Bible together in small groups. The leadership or vestry of the church is encouraged to engage in this work but it is even better if everyone can commit to some form of Bible study. One of my favorite and accessible tools is *Gospel Based Discipleship*. Based on the African Bible Study method and adapted for use in Native communities, this method is both lectionary and liturgically based, and demands no prerequisite education or training. In its simplest form, we engage the gospel through conversation and through community, inviting the Spirit to help us understand what God would have us do today, right where we are. All of the gifts we have are from God and identified in and through community. Native people, often part of the same tribe with similar cultural values and relationship to the land, find that we can see our gifts most clearly as we work together and rehearse together the Creator's stories and look for insight as we discern together. The work of

Bible study is one central step in the identification and honoring of the gifts of each community, and it is also critical to the formation of mission and inclusion strategies.

Throughout this book, I encourage everyone to know that God's desire is to increase the mission and capacity of every community—to use the plentiful gifts that God has given us for the care of the whole world. We do that best when we engage in prayer and Bible study together. When we are able to ask, "What is God calling us to do" and "What gifts do we have to offer?" on a regular basis, not only will our church community be enriched but our whole community and mission will grow. *Gospel Based Discipleship* is available through the Episcopal Church Center website, www.episcopalchurch.org/native.

Attending to Ritual

One of the best ways to encourage the entire church community in this process of inclusion and growth is to consider the liturgy as part of the learning strategy. Using hymns, sermons, prayers, story telling, expressive arts, and other pieces during Sunday and special liturgies can be a very effective method for helping the entire community to engage in this process of identifying gifts and reaching out to others. Various members of your church leadership, along with clergy, church school teachers, and others can create helpful liturgical expressions for this work. The act of inviting folks to consider how to celebrate and reflect the work of the church community within the liturgy (literally, the work of the people) is often a tremendous expansive step on the road to inclusion. Liturgical resources for special events are also available through Church Publishing (www. cpg.org) to augment the creativity in your worshipping community.

Sunday Mornings

Throughout this book, I will call on you repeatedly to be attentive to what is happening on Sunday mornings. Of course, you will be paying special attention to the worship as you grow together, but it is also essential to become aware of what goes on in the rest of the church building on Sundays. You want to begin talking together about what your educational, childcare, and other programs are like. You might want to talk about how newcomers are welcomed to the congregation on their very first visit. In recent years, as I go to visit congregations as a bishop, I have been surprised and sometimes saddened by how folks are welcomed. My husband often travels with me, and although I introduce him to as many people as possible, when he takes a seat in the pews, people will often not greet him. One woman actually turned her back to him when she didn't recognize him and continued searching the congregation for people she could wave at and greet with a word. My husband is attractive, well dressed, and very gentle and unassuming, but there are many congregations that he would choose not to return to because of the lack of welcome for a stranger. If a bishop's spouse, one who knows the service and the Prayer Book, is unintentionally rejected by a congregation, how might a person from another culture or language group be treated? Welcome is so essential to the life and growth of a congregation that I encourage you to educate and train your entire congregation in simple ways to make others welcome in your midst.

Is there something that everyone thinks is great that you do every week? Is there a need you would fulfill, if you had the time, the money, or the personnel? The worship can be spectacular and hearts can be weekly set on fire to follow Christ into the world, but if there is no childcare, or if there is no thought given to feeding people, the glorious worship can be forgotten quickly. We will return to this issue throughout this discussion, but try to make quick notes as to what might need to be explored, so that when the time comes you will be ready with ideas and plans for a growing future.

Seasonal Activities

The suggested activities at the end of each chapter are best used in sequence, but if they need to be done out of sequence to adapt to the requirements of your church community, please feel free to do so. Creative adaptation is always encouraged, and is actually expected. The intent of the exercises is to spark your church or faith community's creativity and interpersonal engagement. I want you to talk to each other, celebrate one another, play together, and discover God's work in your midst. Congregational development begins when we bring our offerings to God. No matter how humble or complex the circumstances, how limited the resources, or how anxious the community is, there is something that will help you begin to face one another and to welcome those who were once strangers.

The activities throughout this book are designed to involve the broadest possible age range of people. The activities are best done accompanied by a social gathering, party, potluck, or other event that includes food and celebration. Talk and creativity are easier when people feel full and welcome. Remember what it was like when you were a stranger, when you were just starting out, or when you were at a time of having to start all over? The exercises are for all church groups who want to remember what it was like, who are thankful for a welcome and inclusion, and who desire to share God's welcome with others.

EXERCISES

1. **Pictures of Faith:** Distribute disposable cameras to members of the congregation, making sure to include children and elders. Each person is asked to take pictures in response to the question, "What would you want to show someone about our church community?" The younger children might want to draw a picture with markers, crayons, or pencils (some adults might also enjoy making artwork). Schedule a potluck dinner (or some other festivity), where the photos can then be displayed. Ask the gathering, "What stories do these pictures tell about us?" Have someone chronicle the responses. Hint: young people are very good at making videos of gatherings and turning them into DVDs etc.

2. **Tell Me a Story**: Ask some of the elders of the community to tell their stories of the church and community. This can be done as a Christian education project. They can come and sit with children (adults listening in) maybe for 3/4 of an hour and tell their story. Again, have these stories recorded and compiled. Hint: some communities have used the compiled storybooks as fundraisers.

3. If used for the Christmas and Epiphany season, one might schedule a Twelfth Night festival or other festive occasion where stories can be shared and pictures displayed.

CHAPTER TWO

Planting Deep Roots
Grief, Healing, and Sanctuary

(Can be used during Lent, Holy Week and Easter)

I recently visited with the leadership of a small church, which was struggling with how to move forward. Established after the Second World War, this church had flourished for several decades, and then had experienced a slow but persistent decline. The leadership was at the point of wondering if they could keep struggling on. They had recently lost their rector who had been with them for only a few years and who was now going on permanent disability. When I sat with them and listened to their conversation, I realized that this was not the first "clergy shock" that they had experienced, but only the most recent trauma. One former pastor had died in an automobile crash. Another pastor had died after a long bout with cancer, and although he had left the parish several years prior to his death, his loss was still a painful, recent memory. The accumulated pain and grief in the room where we were meeting was overwhelming; and yet they were faithfully trying to press on and serve God in their place.

Their sense of grief was like a blanket over them, shutting out the light and hope for the future. Situated in a community that was changing both in ethnic makeup and median age of residents, it would be easy to look from the outside and say that they were declining and had little hope for a future. They needed some encouragement to see the potential and gifts that were in their midst. They were a community of committed and talented lay people who had suffered, but despite their grief they were able to move on. They challenged themselves to grow and thrive again.

Often we forget that even Jesus took time to weep before he raised Lazarus (John 11:35—"Jesus wept"). This piece of scripture is actually the shortest verse in the Bible and so a favorite of church school children who needed to memorize verses for class in years past. It is also a very personal and pivotal window into the tangible human nature of Christ. Jesus, who stood with the dead man's friends and family, whose hearts were broken by the loss of their beloved, felt deeply and completely their grief and loss. Jesus took time to assess the situation and to acknowledge where they were. Every community, every individual is effected when a trauma happens, whether it's a sudden or protracted death, or a violation of boundaries and trust. Every church community can identify numerous incidents that have caused grief to strike some or all of the members of the church family. We often bury our grief in a false wish to put a positive spin on things, or in the normal desire to make church a happy place for everyone. When we deny what is real in our grief, we deny the heart of God moving among us.

In this chapter, we are going to focus on the incidents that can stand in the way of church growth, and encourage both communal and personal healing in order to open ourselves to the possibility of growth and welcome. Truth is, it is impossible to welcome others and open doors when we are hurting and protective after suffering great losses ourselves. Our natural human reaction to loss and grief is a defensive posture both as individuals and communities. We can only take so much and so we guard ourselves from even the possibility of any new assaults. We can also, inadvertently and unintentionally, guard ourselves from the gifts of new life.

Grief

In one church I worked with, they had the experience of letting go of their pastor after only a few short years. It had been a terrible match between priest and people and nothing either party could do was making any difference. When things ended, there was a great deal of anger. The anger was aimed at the bishop's office, the former rector, and several leaders in the congregation. The sadness felt by this loss and failure was deep grief for what might have been. They had great hopes and expectations and had invested heavily through the clergy search in developing a growing congregation with this priest at the helm. As it is when a family loses a child, all the hopes and dreams for the future may die along with that child. When I went to be with them for the first time after the separation, the rage was very intense, the first wave of their sense of loss. Even if actual death doesn't occur, people may still be plunged into grief, which often displays itself as anger or rage. If you have spent time with a community, you can probably identify a time when this kind of anger spilled everywhere.

In church communities, anger can often be a sign that people are grieving. If you are struggling to revive and grow a community, the real resistance you face might actually be grief in the guise of anger—personal and direct or passive and indirect. Anger is often the first sign that there is some wound within a community that has not been healed. The leadership of a church community can recognize this as bad behavior, which it often is, but also as an invitation to seek healing within the community. Until the wound within the community has been faced and the healing process begun, it may be impossible to continue to grow the church and welcome newcomers.

The first thing I had to learn was that the anger was not really personal or about me, even though it was directed at me. As a bishop, I was a symbol of the church and of authority. When things go very badly, it is entirely human to look to those in authority and blame them for what has gone wrong. I had to let the anger spill out. I had to stand with them and listen to their pain, not taking it personally, but taking it seriously. Bishops and other clergy are particularly prone to wanting to fix that which we did not break, and then are hurt when people blame us for a poor fix for something we didn't even understand. Loving people in the midst of grief demands a gentle patience, which can be very hard for natural caregivers and parental types, like me. Take time to listen and take time to pray with people. The leadership of any parish can make great strides toward healing by simply offering to pray for or with angry, and undone people. Anger and hurt in human beings does not respond well to logic, or even to well thought out remedies. Anger and hurt respond best to compassion and consistency. Human beings need to know that their hurt, pain, and grief is not dismissed, or shunned. A community with the capacity to grow is a community that can accommodate and grieve with individuals, while not taking on their grief, but honoring the experiences and anxiety that they bring to the life of their church community.

In the larger community that surrounds you, there might also be loss and wounds that are systemic and historic. I remember, as a very young child, being told over and over again about the Trail of Tears. In the 1830s, my people, the Cherokee, and several other tribes were forcibly removed from their homelands in North Carolina, Tennessee, and Georgia. They were forced to walk across country in unspeakable conditions to Oklahoma Indian Territory. Of those who were removed and made the long walk, somewhere between 25 to more than 33 percent of the people died in transit. I have an ancestor, who walked each step of the way as a frightened eleven-year-old girl. The Federal Government removed many tribes to Indian Territory and outlawed our traditional ways of worship, dress, and social life. For the exiled Cherokee people, tribal headquarters in Tahlequah, Oklahoma, still embodies their own sense of the sacred, although they are not our original lands. And the tribe has two branches, the one based in Oklahoma and the other in Cherokee, North Carolina (and several other small bands scattered in Georgia). These two groups of people have been working hard to reconnect and reconcile across a divide that was not of their making. We all tell the story of the Trail of Tears in hopes that we will never forget, and in hopes that no government will ever treat human beings like that again. This is part of who were and are, and is necessary to understanding our present and to reshaping our future.

To this day, to some Cherokee people, the wound might have been inflicted yesterday. Those communities, both within and without the church, need to know the historical and ongoing wounds of their common life. Understanding the present day ramifications of slavery, wars, tribal conflicts, segregation, the outlawing of traditional practices—all of these things need to be named and understood. And it is not just minority communities that have experienced catastrophic pain and tragedy. All communities have a story to tell from those who have experienced great suffering through being the victim, being neglected and excluded, or through the damage of living with societal abuse without confronting it and therefore victimizing others, however unintentional that victimization might be. All communities have to face their historical wounds before they can move into the future the God of love has fully planned for all our communities.

I want to share with you a story from an Advent in my life that helps me understand this sense of ongoing loss and the hope for turning loss into healing. In the fall of 2001, several weeks after I had been elected bishop, I was asked by Chad Smith, the Principal Chief of the Cherokee people, to come to Tahlequah, Oklahoma, to speak at a healing service. This was just two months after 9/11, and our whole church and nation, along with the world, was frightened and sad. The folks in Tahlequah, although a great distance away from New York and Washington, DC, were still profoundly affected by the terrorist attacks. Old wounds seemed to be open and the Chief talked to me about the suffering of so many families in my tribal community. I agreed to come and they told me I could bring along anyone I wished. I chose to bring my mother, expecting we could visit family members while we were there. My mother, who is a very proud, beautiful, and faithful Christian woman and a great storyteller, still has some places that are hard for her to return to, even with the prospect of seeing her brother and family. Oklahoma is one of those places, which she loves and yet it can still be very challenging for her. She had to leave Oklahoma as a twelve-year-old child, on a bus, all by herself to stay with relatives in the east, because of alcohol abuse and violence in the family. Growing up, my mother talked very little about her childhood, and we didn't press her. She would sometimes tell us stories, and is in many ways the family historian; but she guards her past as many people do when the wounds are deep.

At the service, the Cherokee Nation's children's choir sang Christmas carols in our language. I was sitting on the podium with other clergy and watched my mother as the service proceeded. My mother smiled throughout, but her face lit up and she had an astounded look on her face while the children sang. When we were finally alone several hours later, I asked her about it, and she told me that she remembered sitting in her aunties' laps and singing these carols in her language and she remembered every word. A lost memory came back to her vividly and she was able to see and remember all the wonderful Christmases she had there as a little girl. From that point on in our visit, she had to show me the site of every wonderful thing she ever did as a small child, and we had to get all the things that meant Christmas to her as a child—especially paper shell pecans. She told me many stories and I got a glimpse of my nearly eighty-year-old mother as a small child, hopeful and full of life. For me, it was the best Christmas gift ever. God opened both of our hearts to receive a great gift. And it was a gift that included new insight and redemption, healing, and honoring of things and people that might have been lost to us both. If we can acknowledge our broken places, we might just be able to find a place for God to renew our ministries together.

So how do we diagnose the hurt? There are a variety of ways to diagnose the pain a church family is suffering. After 9/11, the country saw multiple manifestations of post-traumatic stress syndrome. This was particularly present among those who were first responders, but also among those who were working with first responders. There were critical flare-ups of anger and healthy, long-term relationships started coming apart at alarming rates.

Why did this happen? Because faced with such horror day after day, human beings need a place of relief and sanctuary. Often, the only safe place to take the hurt is home. Church communities are often home-like for many of us and so we act out our pain where we feel most safe. The only way to move beyond the anger is to face the hurt, to acknowledge what has happened and to find ways to honor the grief of an entire community. Some circumstances of grief will need only conversation and recognition to start the healing process, and some situations will call for outside intervention and help from professionals. A church community should never be reluctant to ask for professional help and there is an abundance of resources available through dioceses and other church programs, as well as through local, county, and state government agencies.

Much of the grief in church communities is not as clearly delineated as it was immediately after 9/11. Much of it has been smoldering for years. In order to diagnose the hurt, we have to enlist the help of many people. Churches often fail at moving beyond their "stuck places," because people don't have real opportunities to identify their loss and acknowledge what could have been. As a parish priest, I was confronted regularly by a woman who said she missed "the old ways," the old Prayer Book, and, in her case, the comfort of Morning Prayer on Sunday. The church I served celebrated the Holy Eucharist as the principal service on Sundays and had been doing so for years before I arrived there. It felt like an attack on my integrity as a clergy person and I bristled inwardly when she complained to me after services on Sundays. It felt like criticism and I took it personally. My initial verbal response to her was to tell her that the church had moved on years ago. But her anger and grief were real, and I began to wonder what I could do to help her and others move beyond the loss that she and others felt.

I had to start by listening to her and taking her concern seriously. We established a liturgy and worship group to find ways to provide for a variety of liturgical expressions. We tried several different approaches and styles and then finally found that, if, on some Sunday mornings, during appropriate seasons, I wore cassock and surplice instead of an alb, that visual, liturgical vestment change signified an honoring of the past history of the place and an honoring of her grief. We didn't change everything to the way she remembered it or perhaps thought she remembered it, but we were willing to publicly acknowledge the older traditions, and by doing so, invited her to embrace the present as well as the past. Some grief is not so simple. Some church members are not as clear about what they are grieving or angry about.

Over the past few years, my husband and I have had the opportunity to visit Ireland several times, and have gotten to know a few folks who we have stayed with quite well. On our visits, we have tried to get to know some musicians and artists as we traveled along, as well as visiting churches and clergy in various places—but mostly in the northwest and Donegal. I knew some of the history of the land and people, but was pretty ignorant of the religious history. When we attended several Roman Catholic masses in Gaelic, I was saddened by the lack of music, in a land so rich in music and expression. A woman we stayed with explained that the Roman Catholic Church in Ireland was long outlawed by the English Crown and oppressed by the Church of England, the mother church of the Episcopal Church (in which I presently serve as a bishop). She told us that to openly celebrate mass, a Roman Catholic priest would have risked imprisonment and would travel around after dark. Mass was often said before sunrise, on makeshift altars out in the wilds. She pointed out some of these "altar stones" to us as we toured around with her. They would never sing for fear of being caught and punished, imprisoned, or worse. The countryside is littered with ancient churches that were destroyed during this long siege. This kind of abuse and grief affects the practices of the church in Ireland to this day. The people's music, which is lively and expressive everywhere else, is barely found within the walls of the church. Knowing the community, the people, and their history is essential to congregational development.

The cardinal rule in this process is to ask, don't guess. The leadership of any church can find ways to ask people to respond to their own sense of loss. During an appropriate season, Lent and Holy Week (or Advent) are particularly appropriate, a group can begin to ask people to respond to specific questions. The group can draw up their own community-specific questions, and it is appropriate to keep these questions simple—but invite a variety of ways to answer them.

- What one thing about our church gives you great joy? What one thing upsets you?

- Who (in this community) has affected your life positively? Who has challenged or discouraged you? (This can also be asked of programs.)

- When have you felt most inspired? When have you felt reluctant to participate?

- How can we encourage each other better? How do we need to change to do that?

- What should we pray for in the coming days?

When asking a group of people questions, the leadership should expect a large range of answers. The questions you asked can be put to people in a forum, a church school class, or during a dinner gathering or social event. Remember though, many people are reluctant to openly voice their sadness. Some others might not trust or know the community well enough to feel free to respond. Everyone can have the opportunity to answer the questions in writing and anonymously. This allows the leadership to hear the widest range of information. And don't leave the children out of this process; they are often more honest and sensitive to the grief swirling around them than the adults.

This survey of the heart can go along with other spiritual exercises that folks might take on in Lent. The final question about prayers could be used to format prayers and intercessions for the season. The answers to the questions might also guide the leadership to design liturgical expressions that could invite healing and reconciliation for an entire community. The range of grief in any give community can be enormous and some situations may need immediate professional help. Some other situations can be dealt with by designing services of remembrance, or making a history project that connects the past to the present—while opening the doors to the future.

Healing

The first step to healing is to acknowledge the hurt. "There were two blind men sitting by the roadside. When they heard that Jesus was passing by they shouted, 'Lord, have mercy on us, Son of David!' The crowd sternly ordered them to be quiet, but they shouted even more loudly, 'Have mercy on us, Lord, Son of David!' Jesus stood still and called to them, saying ' What do you want me to do for you?' They said to him, 'Lord, let our eyes be opened.' Moved with compassion, Jesus touched their eyes. Immediately they regained their sight and followed him." (Matthew 20:29–34)

The blind men were aware of their need and even though the crowd wanted to silence them, they acknowledged their lack, their hurt, their need, and Jesus responded to their need with compassion. Every community of faith has hurts, injuries, and other pains that accumulate over many years. These compounded injuries have left many sitting by the roadside, like the two blind men, unable to move on, unable to follow Jesus. There is no shame in asking for the help we need from one another, and there is no shame in asking God for what we need. Jesus directly invited the blind men to be clear about their need. Jesus invites all of us to be clear about what we need, whether we are asking on behalf of communities, individuals, or families. The questions that were just presented might help folks identify their needs and the real "vision" problems within the community.

In the gospels, healing takes place through Jesus' touch, or through the touch of his disciples. Most healing, whether individual or communal, is effected through some means of touch. Lent is an appropriate season to begin a healing ministry in which an entire parish community can participate. Healing, being "hands on," might elicit hands as symbols and expressions.

I served in a parish where the children of the community had provided the basis for a church—a wide healing tapestry. They made their handprints in different colors of washable paint on a long strip of white fabric that then decorated sanctuary, parish hall, and church-school rooms. Adults and children alike would write and draw on this fabric (with markers) their prayer requests and needs. One part of the tapestry was made into a stole for the clergy as a reminder to all that Christ's hands were our hands and that we could all participate in healing and reconciliation. Prayers for healing might be offered as part of the Sunday services, or a separate weekday service might be scheduled for healing. In the BCP (pages 458–461) there are a number of prayers for healing that can be used at home. Some parishes find that offering the Reconciliation of a Penitent (BCP 447ff) as a community service toward the end of Lent or during Holy Week, can be a helpful tool for many. There is no one way to encourage healing in a parish but moving from grief to healing is essential when communities desire to become places of welcome and invitation.

Grief, pain, and loss are part of the healing process and when we acknowledge our pain and anger we can face God and one another and open ourselves to the healing God constantly offers us. When I was a relatively new mother with an eighteen-month-old daughter, I was hospitalized for surgery to correct a herniated disc in my lower back. Mark and I had just moved to Denver, Colorado, several months earlier and we knew very few people there, save for the people he was working with in the theatre. We had attended church, but were new enough to not feel secure in the community we had temporarily joined. As you might imagine, it was difficult for me to leave my little one for several days, but my mother agreed to come out to Colorado from New York while I was in the hospital to care for our daughter. The surgery was scheduled late in October and things seemed to go along as planned. Several days after the surgery, they found I had a staph infection and determined that I needed to be kept in isolation and remain in the hospital until the infection cleared. This meant that every visitor, including doctors and nurses, had to wear masks, gowns, and gloves, and that I could have no contact with the other patients or with our little one. I was inconsolable and beside myself. I had managed without our little girl for a few days but I was facing possibly a month of dislocation from my child, my husband, and our home. The clergy person from our new church, who had visited once, but was an old friend of the family, refused come into my room, since he had other patients in the hospital. I was angry with God and furious with the world, too.

After many conversations and pleadings, the nursing staff finally let my mother and husband bring my daughter to see me. Nearly two weeks had gone by and I was in agony, not with physical pain, but with the ache of a mother and the dislocation of my life. The rules were clear. To see my child, she would have to wear a gown, gloves, and mask like everyone else. I was thrilled when she arrived and immediately, instinctively, began to pull away mask and gown so I could kiss and nuzzle her baby face. A nurse walked in and began to reprimand me. My little girl, Emily, stood up, with her chubby legs spread on the bed, covered her ears, closed her eyes, and began to scream. The more the nurse fussed at us, the louder she screamed. Finally, after several minutes and no let up, the nurse turned on her heels with a dismissive wave. And immediately, Emily stopped, sat down on the bed, and threw her self at her mother. God's desire for healing in our lives is even more fierce and determined than that little girl. God wants individuals and church communities to resist the routine ways of administering care and replace them with a fierce and compassionate care for community that sees beyond those things that bind us and hold us back. God's heart craves a church that is willing to stand fiercely for love and the care of others.

It was that moment that I consider a turning point for healing in my life. I saw clearly demonstrated in a child, my child, the intense way that God loves us and stands in the breach for us. I could let go of some of my expectations of that time, and let the healing process, both emotional and physical, carry me on to where I needed to be. It was a human demonstration of a divine intention that helped me move from struggling against the situation to a place of openness for new life.

All of us are in some process of grief and healing, all of the time. There is always something to let go, there is always something and someone we must open our hearts and minds to. As members of church communities and, perhaps, church leaders, we have the opportunity to remember that dynamic in all of our congregations, and to be agents of acting and declaring God's fierce love and concern for every being. If we could be less anxious for the small things of each day, we might be able to open ourselves to the people around us who need us to act as God's agents and on their behalf.

Sanctuary

We will return to this subject repeatedly, but at the outset, it is important to be clear about sanctuary. Sanctuary does not only refer to the worship space in a parish, but rather includes the entire communal space. If a church is to become a place of welcome, and if you are serious about church growth, then the church will need to be safe for those who already are part of that community as well as newcomers and visitors. I always like to start out with the most practical of exercises, which I will encourage folks to continue throughout the course of this book. It begins by asking several people, in groups of at least two, to walk slowly through the church facility. One person should record impressions, both positive and negative, about all of the spaces, with special emphasis on kitchen, bathrooms, and nursery. Is this room clean, functional and up to date? Are there things that need to be done? Is there anything that needs to be gotten rid of, thrown away, or moved somewhere else? This is a "walk of first impressions," done by people who know the space. The several groups of people then compare notes about what they saw. These folks might want to prepare a brief report for the leadership and maybe this group, during Lent, might want to do the small things that would upgrade the rooms without much cost. For example, removing all of the old, dirty cloth towels from the kitchen, taking up torn rugs that could trip an older person, and replacing broken towel racks in bathrooms. Of course, more substantive changes should be approved by the vestry and clergy.

Building a safe place for all of the people of a community also requires that the leadership and other adults in the church take responsibility for the safety of all children and young people. Every diocese offers regular training programs for safeguarding children and many require the course work for church-school teachers and youth workers. It is a wonderful, insightful training that every church leader should experience if they are to lead through example. Many parents, too, could benefit from the training as it provides tools and methods for evaluating personal safety in a parish and makes available a wealth of resources for prevention and intervention with any type of misconduct. The leadership can invite growth by honestly assessing the adequacy of safety for both children and adults throughout the community. During a season when we are opening ourselves in a new way to Christ, and opening our hearts to the needs of others, it seems personally and communally appropriate to engage in clear assessments of space and relationships in order deepen our commitment to Christ and to one another.

During Holy Week and Easter, many people visit churches hoping to find sanctuary, a safe place that could provide a sense of belonging and home. Other folks come just to "do" Easter with their family, to fulfill a personal or familial obligation. Whether visitors are coming out of curiosity or obligation, this season can be a wonderful time to reach out and make folks feel welcome. Every visitor to the church community should be able to take home some joyful reminder of their experience of your church. Seed packets with parish contact information attached can be delightful and inexpensive gifts, as well as coloring books and other simple items for children.

It is important to remind folks at this stage, that if in the process of examining a church community for unresolved grief, unsafe environment and practices, and other configurations and relationships that may need healing, critical or serious issues might arise that need professional help. There are an abundance of resources available through your diocesan office and other church structures. Long buried secrets are painful to face anytime, but parish leadership and clergy should not feel intimidated or reluctant if something intense or critical arises. There are many reliable persons, programs, and resources available for the asking. Growing a church will sometimes present challenging circumstances, but a willingness to face whatever comes to us, is a sure sign of sanctuary and welcome to those who might come seeking a family and community of faith.

Before we move on to the next chapter, I want to reiterate how critical this step is to church growth. Grief is a necessary and critical part of human life and relationships. If we bury, ignore, or dismiss our past wounds, we may only have a cemetery remaining. A cemetery is a noble and hallowed place, a place for families to gather at a time of loss and at anniversaries. But it is not a place where outsiders can feel welcome, nor can we expect reasonably that they would be interested in joining with the grieving at graveside. They need to be invited to life and affirmation. They need to be invited to be part of a community that can include them in something larger than themselves, a place where they can witness and experience transformation in themselves and others.

One of the clearest signs of unresolved grief is a church divided into factions, often along extended family lines, where one party is constantly criticizing the others. The outward sign of unresolved grief is a community so factionalized that they are trying to draw outsiders into their fight. When church members are moved to call in bishops, diocesan staff members, and other judicatory heads in to resolve their problems, it is often a sign that some first steps have not been taken. I encourage you to take the time to redeem the grief in Christ. It may take several seasons and several rounds of approach, but ignoring the problem will not work. Facing grief head on always brings with it the promise that God goes with you in the midst of grief, bringing the gifts of healing and transformation into the darkest and most broken places and relationships. God is with you at the foot of the cross and in your darkest hours.

Gifts and Mission

I have suggested that folks take seriously the call to study the gospel together and through this communal conversation with God and one another, seek the specific gifts that a church community possesses and, in turn, help the scripture and the gifts articulate the mission of the particular parish. In each season, it is important to assess whether you are gaining more clarity about gifts and mission.

When serving as a bishop in the Diocese of Newark, I had the opportunity to work with the only Native Episcopal Church in the diocese. The church building was a small white wooden church building that was always in need of repairs. The Ramapo people, who this mission had been set up to serve, have had a multitude of struggles, not only political challenges with recognition by state and federal authorities, but also a host of health and legal issues associated with the reality of having a superfund site as part of their tribal lands. Although situated in one of the most affluent areas of the country, the tribe and people were struggling financially, and they did not have a supportive educational system. The diocese did not have a particularly good relationship with these Ramapo people, and there were real reasons for this group not to trust the capacity of other people to honor them for who they were. When I began to work with them, they seemed overwhelmed with these challenges, and rightly so.

We began simply, by getting to know each other. I came out for a service, prior to Thanksgiving, and we had a meal and conversation afterwards. They talked about all the ways they were trying to help their community. And they shared their deep disappointments with authorities, whether diocesan or local governments. Their priest of several years had left, and they felt that they had been disconnected from the larger church. I asked them if we could keep talking together and find ways to possibly support their ministry. They knew what their community needed, much better than I did and they had some clearly articulated hopes and dreams. My goal was to help us all heal our broken relationships so that we might be able to share some ministry together. They had few economic resources but they had plenty of knowledge and a tenacious desire to see their community thrive and grow. And they had indeed been ignored, misunderstood, and dismissed all too often by well meaning church and government leaders.

We continued to walk, talk, and eat together. After a little over a year, I joined them for a Christmas celebration, in which they provided breakfast and a picture with Santa for the children (of all ages) throughout the community. They fed nearly a hundred people and took as many photos. They raised much of their costs for this event through spaghetti dinners and bake sales (with Native fry bread!) throughout the year. They told me proudly that one thing they knew how to do was to cook and feed people. The leadership of the community had a reputation for tasty food, so people came from all around when they had these fundraisers. They also had youth program, providing some traditional teaching along with food and movies or other entertainment for their young people. They had a large group of children participating, the majority from families who did not attend church regularly.

In our ongoing conversations, I learned that there had been a group of people, women primarily, that had been making traditionally patterned and quilted stoles, but that this community based development project had ceased after funding cutbacks that came after 9/11. There was some genuine sadness and anger for one more project so quickly abandoned. With their permission, I was able to connect them with the diocesan altar guild, which helped them finish the stole project. There were over a hundred stoles all told and many of them had actually been finished. The leadership of the diocesan altar guild and the diocesan staff made these stoles available for sale, with the proceeds returning to the community for their programs. With the additional funds they have begun setting up an after-school program in their parish hall, so that children in their community have help with homework and other remedial assistance. They will continue to teach traditional arts and stories through this program, as well as providing employment and training for several people in their area who have been without work and have been profoundly under-employed for years. This community, with very limited financial resources, is a place where there is abundant creativity and encouragement for new projects and ministries. Despite continuing legal struggles, their care for one another and the young people provides encouragement for the larger church. And they are making a positive impact on their community despite the collected grief and disenfranchisement they have suffered over many generations.

Are their people and ministries that have come to light in the past weeks? Are there areas and groups that seem to be providing hope and encouragement for others? Is there someone or something you are excited about? In the midst of this season, where you have faithfully examined the collective grief and begun the work of healing, you are encouraged to recognize and celebrate the positive changes that are already happening in your community. If there is something or someone to celebrate, I encourage you to take time during a Sunday service to recognize that gift in your midst. The more we can celebrate the blessings God has bestowed upon us, the more likely we are to truly see them.

Attending to Ritual

It is important to incorporate the learning and growth that your community is encountering through ritual, liturgy, or other visible and visceral expressions of God's activity in your life as a community. Every church community has different ways of expressing grief and change, so remember to consider including in the liturgy aspects of the learnings that have happened during this chapter or season. From a simple choice of hymns that really speak to the heart, to sermons that address issues head on, the liturgy, as work of the people, can help everyone express their inclusion in the bigger story of God's love. The love of God is present with them in their grief and changes, in their healing and opening to growth.

It is always advisable to have a group of people helping to plan the liturgies of the church. This group can create together a richer tapestry than one person could by himself or herself. In the Episcopal Church, it is expected that the rector of a parish is responsible for the liturgy, but this does not mean that they are exclusively responsible for the liturgy. Inviting others to plan and dream with the clergy and musician(s) is an invitation to trust and responsibility. Sharing leadership whenever possible expresses to everyone that they are critical and necessary to the life of the church community. If we can find ways to lift up shared leadership so that all the people of the community can see and understand it, the growth achieved will be nurtured and deepened.

Sunday Mornings

The church leadership and others have already begun to look at the parish with a different lens and so it is important to reflect on the activities and space use of Sunday mornings. Maybe one of the parents with young children might want to check in with other parents and find out what they need on Sunday mornings. It might be time for the ushers to ask those who come into the sanctuary or who use the facilities on Sunday mornings about their experiences and their needs. Do people stay away for any reason? Is there a group that they are a part of that might want to have a program on Sunday or some other day? Remember that this reminder about the use of the space and the programs provided is to prompt the congregation to look at the space and time you have with others as a gift. A real gift is treasured and accommodated so that everyone can enjoy it. The common space and time you share is a holy present from God, both familiar and mysterious. The more ways you can take time to discover the mysteries of your shared gifts—especially the space and time on Sunday mornings—the more God's activity will be revealed to the community. This also provides opportunity for others to witness God in the midst of community.

What follow are some exercises that your parish or community can try to help work through the grief process. There are many other techniques available as well.

EXERCISES

1. **Eggs.** During the church service folks are given a plastic egg with a slip (or slips) of paper inside. They are asked to write down their pain, grief, sorrows—those things they want Christ to transform in their lives. They are invited to bury the egg, in a drawer (or some other place where they will remember it later) for the season of Lent. They are invited to pray about these relationships, people, and things, turning them over to God whenever they come to mind. At Easter, people can bring forth their eggs to decorate the church and are given slips of paper to write and place on a flower decorated cross (Styrofoam). These are the risen signs of all the broken things that were buried. Since many of the things written are very personal, what gets hung on the cross does not need to be words but could be signs and symbols, known to the church members themselves.

2. **Clay.** This suggestion comes from the Rev. Janet Broderick from Grace, Van Vorst in Jersey City, New Jersey. She has, during Lent and other times, given parishioners a piece of clay to mold while the service is going on, asking them to transfer their grief, loss, and their prayers to the clay in some form. She fires these figures in a kiln and they surround the parish during Lent as a reminder of all that they are offering up to God for healing and transformation. They come to the cross during Holy Week and become part of the flower arrangements for Easter. If some people are put off by clay, due to mess, etc., there are other modeling compounds that can be used and are easily found in crafts stores.

CHAPTER THREE

Exploring and Mapping
Telling the Story
of the People

(Can be used during Pentecost)

The work of this season is the some of the richest, most rewarding, and most sacred work the leadership of any community can do. I also consider the work of this season as the most fun. Discovering a new world in the midst of the most familiar surroundings is both challenging and rewarding. You should also expect this work to be more time-consuming and labor-intensive because it is critical to the next steps towards church growth. In many senses we will be on a treasure hunt for the gifts and riches your community possesses.

When I was a child, I often was at loggerheads with my teachers when it came time to talk about explorers and discovery. "Columbus didn't discover a new world, we were already here!" I would argue at length with my teachers that although we celebrate the gifts of those who explored and conquered this hemisphere, our Native people were farming, hunting, trading, and establishing governments here long before Columbus, Pizarro, the Pilgrims, and other colonists or any other lost and misguided adventurers decided to set out. Native people were honoring the Creator, God, in and through their daily lives, understanding that all of life was a gift from the Creator. When the gospel was shared, many of my people embraced Christianity as a fulfillment of the Creator's vision for us. Our hearts were filled with the good news. Unfortunately, those who brought the gospel didn't believe our embrace was genuine without our outward dress and styles being changed into their likeness. We had to lose who we were culturally, linguistically, and spiritually if we were convince some missionaries that we were Christians. We were expected to hide the authentic gifts that God had placed in our midst. From a true desire to share the gospel can come an unintentional demand that those who join us in the faith simultaneously join the majority in identity, language, culture, and lifestyle. In effect, this unintentional demand asked that Native people who would join the Christian church lose themselves to the group, and hide their true identities from community. When we do this to those who want to be Christians, we dismiss the incredible gifts that they bring by being who God made them to be. Everyone loses when we exclude the gifts of others because of their "strangeness."

The other earnest mistake that befalls many church leaders arises from their genuine desire to encourage their little congregation. So often, church leaders want to import outside wisdom, purchase other programs and languages to grow and develop their church community. A clergy person or lay leader may have attended a church meeting or conference where the spoken witness to the gospel truly excited them and they want to share it. Human beings are prone to wanting to repeat positive experiences they have had in one place and transfer them to another. They believe that they are augmenting the spiritual experiences of others and want others to gain from their transfer of experience. They assume that other people will respond exactly the way they did. Often this may well not feel like sharing to others in the community—but it may be seen as a true imposition. When we take on something from outside without looking within, we can overlook the real treasures and gifts that are in our midst. We sometimes see with the eyes of conquerors rather than the eyes of the beloved Creator who fashioned us and wants us to use the gifts and encourage those right in our midst. God has planted us in a particular place—not to import the life giving and life transforming gifts—but to encourage and raise them up those gifts right where we are planted; native plants growing in good healthy native soil that calls each plant by name and understands the medicine and the properties offered by each.

In the Cherokee tradition, we have stories of creation and origin that help explain who we are as a people and our relation to the Creator and creation. All traditions possess stories that explain how they came into being and why they live their lives the way they do. Our Cherokee stories were passed down from generation to generation and were also recorded by James Mooney, an anthropologist who came and studied the Cherokees in the 19th century. In our creation story, the sky arch (or heaven) was becoming overcrowded since animals and humans lived together (and worked together) with the Creator. Several animals and birds attempted to reach the watery covered earth but failed. Finally, a spider was lowered with filament attached and was gently pulled back up, drawing the land up from under the oceans that covered the earth. The other beings used the filament to climb down to land, after the turkey buzzard had flown around and around the globe, drying up the land. As the buzzard tired, its wings flapped against the soft earth and we are told that when his wings flapped against the moist ground, our mountains (the Great Smoky Mountains) were formed.

We also are told that there was a first man and woman, Kanati and Selu, who had one son. Their son had discovered a playmate in a boy who mysteriously came from the river. The first man and woman adopted the river boy and tried to tame him but he remained the Wild Boy, the story goes. The two boys were mischievous together, and were profoundly confused by the ease with which Kanati and Selu were able to provide food and clothing for them. They took to spying on the parents. They followed their father and saw that he kept game in a cave in the mountainside, and with quiet conversation negotiated with one animal to be the food for his family. He would release an animal, after much respectful conversation, and kill it with an arrow. The boys were hungry and tried to follow like their father, but did not respect the animals and in the confusion and lack of conversation, all the animals escaped. We are told this is why men have to work so hard to track and hunt for game in the woods.

When they returned home, the boys wanted to eat and so asked their mother, Selu, for food. They followed her, as they had Kanati, and saw that she went to the storehouse for corn and beans. They hid themselves, and saw that she rubbed her belly and corn appeared, overflowing in her basket. Then she rubbed her armpits and an abundance of beans appeared. The boys were shocked and decided that she was evil and needed to be killed. Somehow she overheard their plan and told them that if they were going to kill her, to make sure that they drag her body seven times in a circle and then seven times across the ground inside the circle so that there would be plenty of corn and beans for all. They did kill her, and tried to follow her instructions, but tired from all of the work and only cleared part of the ground. From her blood droplets, corn plants sprang up, but in small patches where they had dragged her. This is why, our elders told us, we have to tend our crops carefully and plant twice a year, with much labor.

I share with you this creation story with you to encourage you to see that every people, every language group, and every nation or tribe, has in their history a story of their origins and some rationale for roles and work in their community. Many of the stories we call myths give us great insights into the nature of human beings and their relationships with one another, all of creation, and the Creator. The centrality of creation stories point to the need for all of us to know how we got here, and what continues to motivate us. These stories help us to form an understanding of our place in the world and in the communities and families in which we live. We are all influenced by the stories of our origins, whether it is ancestral, familial, religious, or tribal. I encourage everyone who is engaging in this work to learn their own traditional stories, if they do not know them, or to share their stories, if they do. I will invite you to do the work of an anthropologist, in this next section, but I also encourage you to know the perspective and stories that you bring to the conversation and discovery. You might find you learn as much about yourself as you do about your broader community.

We, as church leaders and regular human beings, often focus too heavily on the side of one or the other—insiders or outsiders. We focus too much on bricks and mortar and pre-serving what we have; or we focus on a mission thrust and cel-ebrate everything that is done in exotic and foreign places, ignoring or shortchanging the needs of our own people. The intention of this book is to honor what is in our midst, while expanding our capacity to reach out in mission and the inclu-sion of others. To accomplish this, I want to encourage folks to borrow techniques from cultural anthropologists and other sci-entists who act as participant/observers in their research. The leadership of a church community has very specific roles with clear and regular tasks that demand time and attention. These roles and tasks do not in any way exclude them from under-standing the unique and complex community to which they have been called. When I refer to community, I am referring to the wider community in which a specific church is planted. Are we in a city, a town, a village, a suburb? What commerce, indus-try, and organizations significantly impact our lives as a whole? What are our local politics, demographics, cultures, and ethnic make-up? Some techniques can be very helpful in understand-ing where we are planted and how we are effected by where we are. Qualitative research methods borrowed from academics can be quite helpful in this process.

"Qualitative research properly seeks answers to questions by examining various social settings and the individuals who inhabit these settings" (Berg, 1998:7). Berg explains that in tak-ing the concept of symbolic interaction from Blum, qualitative research provides a platform for understanding and getting to the meaning of leadership that is found in this specific commu-nity. A research methodology had to be selected that could aid in unearthing the complexity of interactions that occur in this unique place, and a qualitative approach seemed to provide the most adequate tools for the task. Qualitative research allows us to "fully grasp the meaning of a change in their lives for particular persons by developing a description of life quality that allows the interdependent parts of quality to be integrated into a whole and placed in context" (Patton, 1990: 49).

The qualitative research approach design can best be described as an ethnographic field study. Bruce Berg writes that, "the term 'analytical ethnography' refers to research processes and products in which, to a greater or lesser degree, an investigator

(a) attempts to provide generic propositional answers to questions about social life and organization;

(b) strives to pursue such an attempt in a spirit of unfettered or naturalistic inquiry;

(c) utilizes data based on deep familiarity with a social setting or situation that is gained by personal participation or an approximation of it;

(d) develops the generic propositional analysis over the course of doing research;

(e) strives to present data and analyses that are true;

(f) seeks to provide data and/or analysis that are new; and

(g) presents an analysis that is developed in the senses of being conceptually elaborated descriptively detailed and concept-data interpenetrated" (1998:120).

The reality of this type of research is that "the practice places researchers in the midst of whatever it is they study" (Berg, 1998:121). This ethnographic style of qualitative research is intentionally comprehensive and rich in cultural description, as well as providing some contextual and cultural translation.

The purpose of understanding a research method for collecting information about a particular church community is so that we can create new sets of lens and eyes with which to view who we are and where we are going. Many church leaders think they fully understand who they are, who's in charge, and what factors influence decision making in their church and local community. Without taking the time to step back, observe, and gather, we cannot know ourselves truly and therefore cannot know how to expand who we are and what we do to include others. Inviting growth means inviting an honest and clear assessment of our collective lives.

You are encouraged to use every available method (non-invasive) of collecting information from people in your community. In this digital age, there are a variety of methods for recording and storing information. This stage of your work is focused on exploring and mapping—at it's most simple—opening your eyes and seeing; opening your ears and hearing. There is an incredible story of the people who surround us but we are often too busy with the daily and weekly tasks of life to truly know ourselves and our neighbors. This is a time of finding your personal story within the larger story of your church community, and likewise knowing the church's story in the midst of the wider community.

When I was a child, my Cherokee grandfather came to live with us and told us children many stories from his growing up years in Oklahoma Indian Territory. I share the following story, before we move on to exploring and mapping, in order to show the unique ways communities work and how important it is to take time to learn the unique narrative reasoning of the place in which you are trying to do ministry. The following words are my grandfather Ralph WalkingStick's actual words, as he made a tape (with my father's help) for all of us, so that we might remember to tell our children his stories.

> We had loads of fun, particularly the youngsters, when a couple got married. The groom was, by tradition, supposed to have a hog, horse, or cow; at least a pair, for a start in life. No on knows how it started, but the groom was supposed to steal these but the bride would be satisfied if he only stole one pig or calf or colt. He naturally got loads of advice on where the fat ones were and how easy it would be to steal them. His clos-

est friend was in on the deal with their neighbors, but would not let on to the groom as to what trick on him was "in the offing." The point was to keep the groom from stealing anything; thus holding up his marriage. He didn't want that.

The friend told him where a nice hog would be bedded down after dark, and also told the conspirators. When the poor groom, after stalking along through the woods, up and down hills, across creeks and sometimes crawling on his belly to avoid men out looking for him, he would arrive at the spot where the animal was supposed to be. The woods and tall grass around would erupt with yelling, shooting Indians bent on capturing him, but not hurting him. Sometimes they captured him but most times the groom was so scared that nothing could have caught him. This business might go on for a month with the poor guy trying harder all the time. Then the conspirators would tire of the game and let him steal an animal. The owner would go around groaning and bewailing to high heaven the loss of the very valuable animal. He was ruined now for life. He would starve. His family would starve, but when he looked over the stolen animal he could never recall ever seeing it.

I share this story in this place to remind us that every community and family has ways of being together that no outsider can understand. Often, even the insiders don't understand why things happen the way they do, and why certain traditions are observed. My grandfather often remarked, "nobody knows how it started," or "that was long before my time." These very common words can be clues that you might just be discovering something sacred and iconic to the life of the community. Take notice of those moments when people say things like, "we have always done it that way." More than just a way of dismissing the question concerning why something is done, this can be an indication that the activity had some significance long ago and has become bedrock to the life of the community, or to at least to some in your church family. That doesn't mean you must tiptoe around the particular ritual or information, but rather, you should take seriously the central nature of the ritual or symbol, and make sure that it is lifted up and discussed by as many people in the community as possible.

Exploring

"After this, the Lord appointed seventy-two others and sent them, two by two, ahead of him to every town and place where he was about to go. Jesus told them, 'the harvest is plentiful, but the workers are few.'" (Luke 10:1–2)

This is the beginning of a great and profound gospel story, where Jesus sends 72 unidentified people and they return with great joy. Jesus has given them power to encounter others, share the gospel, and to bring healing into the lives of others. These 72 people were expected to be part of the communities that welcomed them, talking with families and individuals, sharing their food and participating in the routines of the people's daily lives. They had to get into the midst of folks and know them so that God's power and transformation might take place in peoples lives. The 72 returned with joy, although many probably started out with fear, facing the unknown with no money, no reservations, and no spare food. In our many of our present day churches, we are strangers to the surrounding communities, outsiders to the environment where we worship, and wonder why there is no power, growth, and transformation in our church. We don't know who is in our neighborhoods and yet we want reservations, plans, and well-packed bags in order to go out and meet our neighbors.

To all of our anxiety about stepping out, and this anxiety is real to many, Jesus says to us, as he said to the 72, "the one who listen to you, listens to me, and the one who rejects you, rejects me." (Luke 10:16) Whenever we are sent out to seek and share the gospel in our lives, Jesus goes with us as our strength and companion on the way. The work we are undertaking in this part of the chapter will come in two "steps." The first step will be off the curb, a walk through the neighborhood, town, the highways and byways, as we seek Jesus' healing and transformation for ourselves and for our community. I like to call this part of following Christ's great commission as *exploring in faith* or *walking the world to find Jesus.* In the season of Pentecost, we are people seeking to welcome and understand God's power in our lives. We are seeking the Holy Spirit's indwelling so that we might get busy for Jesus. Part of the task of welcoming God's Spirit and getting active for God, is having a real curiosity about where we are and who we are in community. This is the season to become happy explorers, kids on an adventure, seeking God in our midst as we turn over the rocks in our towns and villages. Sometimes we get too busy to know where we are. In this season we are called to learn again intimately (or for the first time) where God has called us (the place), and who we are in our specific community (the people).

The second step or part of the work of exploration feels even riskier. This second phase of gathering insight includes asking outsiders to explore your church community. When I served as suffragan bishop in the Diocese of Southern Virginia, I was caring for many parishes that wanted to grow but had little or no program budget. They wanted help from outside but couldn't afford a parish consultant or someone trained in evaluative work. My staff and I decided to help people model cooperative learning by encouraging several parishes to be consultants to one another. For example, we asked two or four parishes to work together on a simple exploration project. I call this part of the process: *Can I join?* This second phase allows a brief foray from several outsiders from another church in the communion (but is not strictly limited to the same communion) who can give clear and useful information, which could not otherwise be gathered. It can also encourage leadership from several churches to share ideas and feedback in a non-competitive way. When all of the participating churches have become actively involved in the process, it begins to seem less of an invasion and more of an exercise in cultivation and insight.

Phase One: Exploring in Faith or Walking the World to find Jesus

In order to explore, I think it is best to have teams of at least two people willing to travel the streets together. This is not only a good gospel idea, but it can encourage two sets of eyes, two sets of ears to see and hear more than a single person could. God is always in the midst of community (whenever two or three are gathered) and so to walk the streets seeking God is to take a friend along. Obviously, few churches have 72 volunteers or twelve teams to do the exploration. Even three or four teams can accomplish incredible learning when taking on the task of exploring community. It is best to take plenty of time to do this exploration, stopping as necessary for meals and conversation, seeking in all ways to engage the people around you. This might be a project that is done over several weeks. Some folks might decide to do the exploring on spring evenings, while others may take daytime or late night explorations. There is much to be gained from having the broadest picture of the world around you. Ideally, there would be a mixture of ages and genders represented in the teams. However you construct your teams, try to have the broadest possible range of folks represented, because we each see different aspects of our community depending on our age, gender, and economic background. The richest insight comes when a new set of eyes sees a familiar experience and someone else has the opportunity to explain what is going on. There is always richness in diversity and insight is gained when many people across a wide spectrum compare notes and impressions.

Here is a list of suggested questions that might be helpful as you walk your community.

- What businesses are in your community?

- Who has authority in your community?

- What do the houses look like?

- Are there visible problems?

- Are there hidden things you discovered?

- Where do people congregate?

- Who gathers where and when?

- Where is there poverty, wealth?

- When were you scared?
- When did you feel safe?
- Are there things that seem dangerous?
- Are there things that surprise you?
- Who did you meet on the road?
- What did you learn from them?

Phase Two: Can I Join?

Church leaders from two or four parishes get together to work on helping each other understand their churches better. The folks decide on a time line in which explorers from another church can come unannounced for a Sunday visit, and a time when they can have access to the church to take photos of the property. They are asked to take ten to twelve photos of each other's churches to include:

- outdoor signs
- walkways and parking lots
- sanctuary or worship space
- entrances
- offices
- parish hall or other gathering place
- church school rooms
- nursery, kitchen
- bathrooms
- indoor signage

These same observers would come on a Sunday morning, acting as newcomers to the community, at random, observing how newcomers are welcomed and all other aspects of interactions between church members, clergy, children, and elders.

These outside explorers could make a simple report on what they liked or didn't like; how they were treated; and what things they might like to incorporate into their own Sunday morning church routine. Their photos could prompt simple observations about what they felt the prominent symbols in the church were, who was in charge, who was being invited to participate, who was being kept away, and what they liked and disliked most about the church space.

Presentations

Once everyone has scheduled the exploration adventures, walked and returned, it is important for the church community to hear about what the explorers learned. The presentations should also include the "outsiders," making personal presentations. I have found that it is easy to discount written observations as they can seem cold and calculating, but someone from another church community, who would take time to participate, look, and assess, is most often received as a beloved missionary and a friend in the gospel. This might be done on a Sunday morning, during the service presentations, or as a coffee hour chat, or in the context of as a festive and fun dinner or barbeque. The presentations could be accompanied by photos or videos, if someone was so inclined and had the equipment, or could simply have local maps outlining in different colors the route which each of the explorers took. Obviously, when the outsiders made their presentations, it is helpful to show the photos to the gathering so that people have a visual image of what was observed. I am amazed at how many church members are so familiar with the church hall or office that they fail to observe fire and other hazards that are right there in front of them.

If you are engaging this process during Pentecost, the longest part of the church year, the gatherings and the presentations should be scheduled at a time when people are going to be in church, rather than during standard vacation times. Often the exploring pieces (walking the community and the photos especially) can be done during light attendance times, but to get an accurate assessment, visits and presentations should be done when the "outside" explorers can see programs in process, can understand fully the measure of the church community, and as many people as possible can benefit from the observations.

Attending to Ritual

It is important that these explorers be officially sent out, and received back in, for they are doing Christ's ministry in the community. We remember from the Luke's gospel story of Jesus sending the 72 out that this was an anxious and holy moment for them. Anyone who willingly undergoes a mission on behalf of the larger group needs the support of the group as a whole. Whether you have only two groups going out or ten, these folks are risking much by exploring the familiar. They are opening themselves to dangers—from personal and spiritual vulnerability to the reality of walking a community that has only been observed for the most part from the safety and distance of an automobile. Very few of us engage in these kinds of intimate journeys, and when we undertake exploration, we need to sense and know that a whole community of people stands behind us.

A simple commissioning service from Lesser Feasts and Fasts can be used to send them forth and welcome them back. One of the explorers might want to write a prayer for this time of discovery and exploration. And the children of the church community might be asked to make badges for the explorers or some other official symbol of their commissioned status. These rituals might seem to be small things, but together, they point to a church community willing to risk change and observation in order to grow and transform. It is not a small thing for a church community to acknowledge their dependency on another church. The relationship with the outside observers needs to be recognized and honored, and they should be included in the prayers, the commissioning services, and any other ritual or signage that you create for this phase of the process.

Mapping

Now that all of the information is gathered from the explorations, something needs to be done with it. On my mother's wall there is a reproduction of an old map dated about the mid-seventeenth century, and even an untrained eye can see that things are terribly out of scale compared to modern maps. My children and visitors to her house have often commented on the way the Americas are depicted as overly large, while other continents are either undersized or misshapen. They also notice that the perspectives and relationships are all wrong. Maps are a gathering of collected information from explorers and this map contained the current perspective and accumulated knowledge of the explorers and the mapmakers they employed to accompany them. When we set out to explore and map our community, we bring with us our own perspectives and our accumulated knowledge of the relative size and importance of individuals, businesses, and organizations.

During this phase of mapping, be reminded at the outset that even professional mapmakers have to work with the limited knowledge and information they have gathered. This is not so much an exercise in getting everything right as much as collecting and drawing rough pictures of your community based on the information you have gathered. We are fortunate in these days to have satellite imagery, onboard automobile computers for exact directions, and other exacting scientific devices that can show us the minutest details of the Earth's surface. Remember, though, that this is not an exacting exercise but an exercise in understanding and exploring relationships. The task deals with our relationship to God, our relationships with one another, and the way we relate to our neighbors. We are trying to understand the garden in which God has planted us, and through that understanding, are learning how to deepen and strengthen our church community so that it might grow and flourish.

The first step in mapping is to purchase (or download) a detailed map of your community. In the exploring segment of this exercise, you may have already outlined the routes and other details from the explorers' journeys. There are several things you want people to understand in a very visual way. Everyone in the church community can be invited to identify where they live and how far they travel to go to church. This can be done over several weeks, with each family given a sticker, dot, or other emblem to place on the map. Make sure a visual list is kept posted in a central place that identifies the family and individuals' names and the distance they drive or walk to church. Again, their routes can be drawn with colorful markers and highlighters, if that helps. The purpose of this is to begin the mapping process with the people who have a defined and clear relationship with the church. If the routes from their homes to the church are drawn in, there may appear to be a spider's web growing on the surface of the map. This visceral understanding of the complexity of the present community becomes the basis for understanding and integrating the complexion and complexity of the surrounding community.

The explorers will have gathered a great deal of information, and may want to come together, after the initial presentations, to distill the information they have shared. Remember to consider messiness as a sign of God's presence with us. There is an old song that says, "God troubled the water," and God continues to trouble the waters and make our lives appear surrounded by mess. The tendency to simplify the information is normal, but be on the watch for the things that disturb or trouble you most. These "outsiders" might bring a great deal of insight into the community and the church. When the explorers gather with the church leadership, honesty and candor need to be welcomed. Growth cannot happen if everyone is afraid to tell the truth. This is most often a joyful process, with many "ahas!" arising as folks compare notes and observations—but don't' be put off if things get uncomfortable from time to time. We are dealing with people and relationships, so expect a little anger with discovery and know it to be God stirring the waters. God troubles our hearts on occasion, so that we might see more clearly and be called into deeper relationship with God and one another.

At this point, there is a good deal of raw material to compile. The summer season is a good time for several groups or individuals to take the raw materials and find ways to present them to the church leadership. The church leadership, vestry and clergy together, should take these observations seriously and begin to help tell the story of the church and community.

Location

One of the gifts of our times is that anyone can get a very accurate map of almost any community. Google provides satellite images of most areas and these maps can be downloaded and displayed for all to see. But these same maps cannot define how you came to be in your location and why you are worshipping on this spot. This is a good time to republish a parish history, if there is one, or get to writing the parish history if there has not been one. Often there is one member of the community who has compiled a great deal of information and with little more than a prompting invitation can set out that history. Every aspect of why you are where you are is important—so don't overlook confusing or complicating historical details. Having a history, which includes pictures and stories from the past, can help deepen the sense of belonging to your particular church location. This gathering of history can be a fertile ground which defines where you once were and who you once were. It can also seed a new sense of identity, which is breaking forth as you move forward.

Identity

Understanding the unique identity (identities) of the people in your church and in your community is essential to making space for newcomers. This is the time to take note of the culture, place/country of origin, racial make-up, and ethnic background of you and your neighbors. Are we all from similar backgrounds, or very different ones? Have people been here for generations or are people from somewhere else? Who do they consider leaders and who do they look to in times of trouble? Where do they place the highest value? These and other questions can help you as you form a better understanding of the identity of your community.

For example, if the majority of your community places a high value on children, do you have programs in your church that respond to that value? In some communities, programs are offered for individual or personal development while the community itself places a higher value on community development and collaborative leadership. This is particularly true in Native communities. Listening for the cultural and spiritual values of the community is an essential part of the work. Along the way, you may be surprised by members of your wider community who have rich and exciting stories to tell, which can shed light on the need for new ways to express the gifts that are scattered across your town or village.

You may want to find creative ways to display the varieties of people, language, cultures, and values that are represented in your church community and your town. Are there symbols of your life together that can be displayed? Obviously, the local sports teams might be part of the local identity, but are there flags from other countries or other symbols of who you are collectively that can help with the mapping of a community? Find ways to make visible what may have been hidden from view for too long.

Factors you might want to pay special attention to are the indicators of roles and occupations that appear across your community, and the ways in which those roles are depicted in various places. This is a central issue in understanding identity in community. When I was a child of twelve, I was diagnosed with a tumor in my abdomen. In the mid-1960s, the technology being what it was, my parents feared that I had some form of cancer. Medical testing has come a great distance from that time, and I am pleased to report that I had a benign but very large tumor that was removed, along with some intestine and my appendix. The hospital stay was quite protracted in those days, more than two weeks, and I was sedated most of the time.

One Sunday, while I was sleeping, a visitor came to my room. When I awoke, I saw a sweet-faced older man, dressed in a white and gold pointed hat and a robe of the same brilliant fabric that reached all the way to the floor. He carried a long gold staff in his hand and seemed to be leaning on it for support. The light filtering in through the window made his outfit even more dazzling. My first impression was that I had died and this was the famous St. Peter, welcoming me to heaven. Remember, I was twelve and a Presbyterian. As I gained a little more consciousness, I heard another person in the room and turned my face to see a Roman Catholic priest who was introducing me to the Cardinal Archbishop of New York. My father was very involved in the ecumenical movement and had many clergy friends across the area from many different communions. Cardinal Spellman spoke briefly to me and told me he had been visiting the hospital and had a service in the chapel. While he was here he wanted to meet Don's daughter. He was very kind to me, and said a prayer for me and then blessed me in his tradition. I was mightily impressed, even though I was only half awake at the time. Now that I am a bishop in another communion, I often wear a cope and miter, but in those days, I had no idea about liturgical vestments, what they stood for, or who wore them. As you do the listening and collecting, remember to ask about roles and how they are designated and symbolized. It is often too easy to make assumptions about dress, vestments, and other indicators, that we might misunderstand, if we do not ask for clarification.

Practice

What communal practices point to the identity of your community? Are there celebrations that are significant for everyone in your town, or are there certain celebrations that are specifically focused on one group? You might also look at the services and celebrations that are important to the life of your church community. Are there certain feast days, times of year, or annual events that are critical to your identity? I am talking about the services that draw old friends and neighbors, or those which generate lots of anxiety or discussion at vestry meetings or among the leadership and people alike. Understanding the practices of the community and the church help us to determine whether there are points of intersection, and whether there might be strategic ways a church could honor and include more of the community's life within the life of the church. Again, finding ways to make visuals with the materials you are collecting helps everyone engage the process of growth.

Mission

Mission is what we do. And what do we do as a church community has an incredible effect on the wider community and its sense of welcome and inclusion. Is your church one that goes outside to do mission and service? Have you collaborated with others to do service and mission and do you provide space and support for various community services? How many of members of your church volunteer in local non-profits and outreach? It is important to identify and acknowledge the non-profits and service organizations in your community. You might want to develop relationships with these agencies to understand the types of services that are provided within your region, and also to be aware of the needs in the community that are presently going unmet. This activity is not meant to be a report card, nor is it meant to be a judgment. Often, when we engage in understanding the missions we participate in we learn that our church is very active. We can identify people with gifts and skills to celebrate and we can encourage others to get involved by matching them up with others in our church community who are already involved with a specific cause.

The leadership of a church community has a critical role at this stage in the process. As people who love and know your church, they can sort through all this material, all these patterns and maps, all of the things that have been discovered, and try to compile them in a sensitive way. Their goal is to help the church community form a vision not only of the present—but of the future. Some of the information gathered will have to be sorted. First, there may be observations or insights that require nothing more than a simple response. For example, I was recently at a church where the front steps were covered with litter. The regular usher parked in a side lot and came in a side door, and so never noticed the mess. This kind of information does not need to get added to some great findings of parish and community life. Rather, it needs to be added to the list of usher (or other group) duties: clean the front steps when opening the front doors.

You might also have discovered that there are several people who would love to come to church, but they lack transportation. This is not something to hesitate about. Somebody find them a ride! Basic hospitality should not wait for a committee to be formed or a program set in motion. Many church communities have lost the opportunity to have wonderful folks added to their regular worshipping community for lack of someone willing to respond to the basic needs of their neighbors. Go ahead and take those simple actions that could be life changing.

Second, there may be, in the data you have collected, information that is sensitive, for a variety of reasons, or a response or insight that was inappropriate. A mature group of elders (and in a true Native sense that means "the wise ones") should help sort out those things that need not weigh down the wonderful work that has been done during this part of the process

The following charts provide examples of ways to map and diagram your particular church community. They might also help you to see those places where the practice of the church diverges from the local community and where mission and practice can intersect. They are simple diagrams and you are encouraged to make up your own, using your local information as a mapping tool, taking into consideration all the priorities and values that you have discovered in your season of exploring and mapping. These charts and others can help the leadership determine the next stages of the process and how you as a church might engage, welcome, and include others in the life of your church community. To form a simple visual chart of all the materials and information that have been collected, you might ask yourselves these five questions.

- **Location:** What does our location say about who we are in context of our larger community?

- **Identity:** What have we learned about our identity, who we are as the people of God in this place?

- **Gifts:** What gifts have been identified in our community, that benefit both the church community itself and the larger town?

- **Practice:** What events and services do we participate in that engage and respond to the wider community?

- **Mission:** In what other ways are we being called to reach out and serve the broader community?

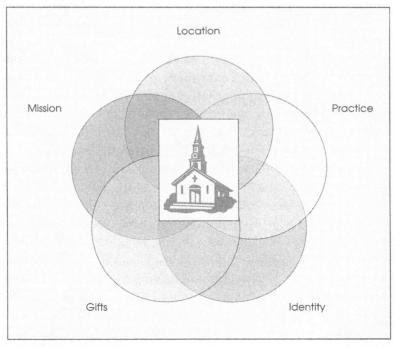

Leadership Strategy Chart 1

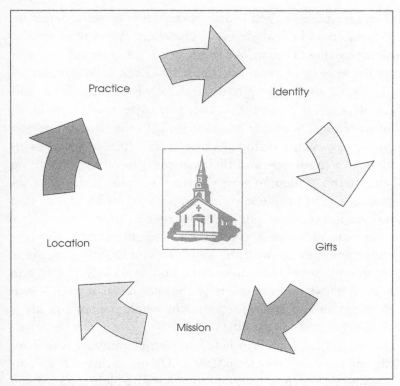

Leadership Strategy Chart 2

Placing the answers to these questions on the following grids or charts (or another chart or picture of your devising) will help the leadership and the congregation with clarity and with planning the next stages of your church growth. As you place the answers on these grids, are there places where your mission and practice intersect? Or seem completely unconnected? Are there places where your location and identity are in stark contrast with one another? Are the gifts we have identified so far being used in our local contexts? Are there people and gifts that have been ignored or covered up that need to be part of our discussion? These are areas of special concern for your leadership to discuss and take seriously.

I recently had a discussion with a man who was complaining about a golf course at a shore location. He expected that every green at every golf course, if cared for correctly, should be as fast as ones he had played on elsewhere. Many of us are the same way about church. We compare them and expect the same results in very different environments. Even if you import all the greens and set it up to a standard, what's underneath still counts, even if it has been hidden by hype, marketing, or an influx of outside people and materials. In the case of this golf course, it was built on top of a marsh. Marshes are always dominant in a landscape and their nature is to return everything built on top of them to marsh status. The same is true for congregations and people in your unique location. Make sure that you are not trying to put a golf course on top of a marsh, but rather, are identifying, celebrating, and encouraging the best marsh possible. Some of the most rare and beautiful creatures are found, including birds, fish, and especially plants and grasses native and life giving to that particular region. When these essential partners are gone, the whole structure of life is challenged and can die out.

Your task as leaders or elders in your community is to identify and encourage the local flora and fauna to thrive. If we participate, rather than try to dominate that which is native and local, we are more likely to flourish and encouraging the generations after us to flourish as well. If we try to be something that we are not and pave over the confusing and marshy parts of our common lives, we are likely to be fighting with one another and our own nature and not building for the future.

As a parish priest in Delaware, I was fortunate enough to work with many folks in our community who were excellent observers. One woman, who was the new head of our outreach program, came into my office and asked whether I had ever shopped late at night in the grocery store out by the highway. I admitted I did on occasion since it was open later than the other stores in town and I was forever forgetting something that the children needed for school the next day. She pointed out to me that she had noticed that although her predecessor had said that there were no Latinos in our community, she regularly encountered them in the grocery store and had started up conversations with them. She had found out that several Latino people worked at the horse track nearby, and several others she met worked at the hospital. She began conversations with them, in her limited Spanish, and found out that the people that she talked to worked many late hours and didn't have access to social services in our town because these services were only available during the day. These initial conversations led to relationships and she connected her new friends to the life of the parish, and to the life of the community. Sometimes, it is can be a gift to be forgetful or sleep deprived. God can put us in places and situations that can provide insights for our ministries and new ways of looking at people who are, in fact, our neighbors.

Attention to Ritual

By now there should be a team of people participating in, and planning for the worship or liturgical experiences of the congregation. Ideally, the clergy person (if there is one) does not have to imagine and plan everything, but others are helping to respond to what they are hearing and seeing as the exploring and mapping continues. Some folks like to use the long season of Pentecost, and especially the summer months, to try a new liturgy from a different resource than they have used in the past. The New Zealand Prayer Book and Enriching Our Worship, both provide expressive and alternate ways to pray and worship God together in forms that are still familiar and yet innovative. Creativity in worship does not mean that the forms must be completely original at all times. It might be highly creative in your specific community to simply insert a prayer from a different setting or to alternate the Prayers of the People from the standard usage common to your local parish.

Sunday Morning and Sanctuary

I want to remind you again that part of the role of our church communities is to provide sanctuary and safety. We want to welcome people into a place and a community that will nurture and increase each person's capacity for openness and transformation. Continue to look around your local parish church and see if you can discover other ways to make your church safe and inviting. Are the church-school teachers and the nursery people supported and trained in their ministries? Are there small changes that might make the church building more inviting? For example, is someone in the parking lot (if you have one) helping people with crossing through cars, and bringing children, the handicapped, and others into church?

The conversation that you had earlier with members about the use of space on Sunday mornings is very important at this time. You want to see if there are ways to make Sunday—both the time and space Sunday—a time of grace in people's lives. Are the parents talking and sharing with the leadership about how best to include and provide for the children? Are those people with disabilities and challenges included in the discussions of the use of space, both worship space and other space in the church building? Is there some group that is finding a home in your midst that might be considered when the space is divided up, and when meetings or groups need to be scheduled? The simple task of scanning over some of the information gathered at earlier times might help everyone keep focused on the needs of your community and use the gifts you share to their utmost.

The following exercises could also be offered to the entire church community in order to prepare everyone for the next stages of growth and inclusion. I can't stress enough the importance of the whole church family, and all generations, participating in these exercises. We often overlook some of the most insightful voices when we forget to include the children, the elders, the irregular attendees, and those who wander in by accident or who are dragged in by their parents.

EXERCISES

1. **The Big Picture.** One wall of the parish hall or gathering place might be dedicated to this. A timeline is put up on the wall, long sheets of paper end to end are fine, that displays

the church from inception to present. Everyone in the congregation is asked to bring a picture and place it above or below the time line, near the approximate year they began attending. Make sure to identify each picture with name etc. Families might want to be grouped together. Then other pictures can be added from years past that include people, buildings, celebrations, and other events in proximity to the year they happened. Make sure to leave this timeline up for several months so that it can be added to and corrected. Leave space also to add those who might arrive while you are doing the exercise.

2. **God's Call to Us.** At the front entrance of the church, a simple bare (artificial) tree can be set up with a basket of colorful small clothespins and a basket of paper leaves placed nearby. Most craft stores have some sort of appropriate trees and decorative clothespins. Folks are then asked to write on the leaves a simple one-line answer to the question: "What is God calling us to be and/or what is God calling us to do?" Allow this to be an ongoing exercise for the whole season, and occasionally you can put leaves in the bulletins to remind folks to participate, including those who are visiting. Someone might want to compile what is written on the leaves for the monthly newsletter and the tree might also move around the sanctuary and be a part of the chancel so that folks could pin a leaf on before or after Communion or other service.

CHAPTER FOUR

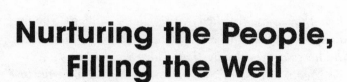

Nurturing the People, Filling the Well

Teaching and Weaving the Stories of All the People

(Can be used during Late Pentecost/fall)

This is a time to congratulate yourself for making the journey so far and for your faithful willingness to open hearts and homes to the transforming love of Christ. Every time we set out to do something new, we set out on a journey of discovery and challenge. You might be feeling overwhelmed by all the information you have gathered. Or you might be thinking that there is too much to take in and not nearly enough people to go around for all the tasks that need to be accomplished. This is the time to remind everyone involved about the blessings you have received so far in this walk by faith. This is the time to find several ways to celebrate your common life in community. There is more work to do, and there always will be, so it is important to celebrate regularly the things that have been done and the people that have made significant contributions to the life of the parish. As you start on each new phase of congregational devel-

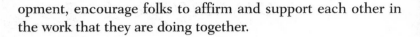

opment, encourage folks to affirm and support each other in the work that they are doing together.

Nurturing the People

"When they were finished eating, Jesus said to Simon Peter, 'Simon, son of John, do you truly love me more than these?' 'Yes, Lord,' he said, 'you know that I love you.' Jesus said, 'Feed my lambs.' Again Jesus said, 'Simon son of John, do you truly love me?' He answered, 'Yes, Lord, you know that I love you.' Jesus said, take care of my sheep.' The third time he said to them, 'Simon son of John, do you love me?' Peter was hurt because Jesus asked him a third time, 'Do you love me?' He said, 'Lord, you know all things, you know that I love you.' Jesus said, 'Feed my sheep. I tell you the truth when you were younger you dressed yourself and went where you wanted; but when you are old you will stretch out your hands, and someone else will dress you and lead you where you do not want to go.' Jesus said this to indicate the kind of death by which Peter would glorify God. Then he said to him, 'Follow me!'" (John 21:15–19 NIV)

I love this passage from John's gospel; for me, it speaks directly to the mission of living for Christ in our local contexts. Peter is discouraged and hurt that Jesus asks him three times about his love and commitment. Although the author of John's gospel tells us that this whole exchange was so that Peter would know about his own death, there is much more to this conversation than just a prediction. In fact, it is the prototype conversation, the big story that we are all a part of and to which we are all called. Jesus wants to know about our love and commitment. And when we are sure about our love and commitment, Jesus would have us nurture and feed those around us. Jesus tells Peter the most intimate secrets of ministry in this passage. He tells Peter that he is and will be totally dependent on others. We are all totally dependent on others, as we do not live and serve God in a vacuum. We live and serve and we are called—to community. Our primary task has remained the same over two thousand years. Jesus says to us all, "Feed my lambs [the young and vulnerable], care for my sheep (my people), and feed my sheep [all of the people, young and old alike]." The repetition is no accident, it is a liturgical reminder, a ritual that teaches us all and reminds us of the central importance in ministry of caring for the health and well being, body, mind, and spirit, of all the people we encounter. Any time we see this kind of repetition, we are being taught, we are rehearsing our lines until they are memorized, we are dancing a dance until we remember each step as part of our being.

The outward sign of our love for God can be found in the way we care and nurture others. Some folks take this piece of scripture literally, and focus their common lives on coffee hour, church suppers, and the like. Others believe that it was a spiritual command and interpret it by placing their focus on bible study and spiritual practices. While both approaches are helpful, I am convinced that the feeding Jesus is talking about is both and more. It is an integrative or holistic approach to the body. It means food, shelter, and encouragement, as well as food for the mind and soul. It is giving people a place and a role in community, while nurturing their gifts and bringing out their best. It is acknowledging the fact that every single person in the community has something to offer and that each of them needs to be fed, watered, and cared for like the true treasure they are. This call from Jesus is an emphatic expectation that everyone is essential to the life and ministry of the community. Everyone has an important part to play. This goes for the youngest to the oldest, the weakest to the strongest, the clergy and laypeople alike.

After my parents retired in the mid-1980s, they moved to a shore community where they had a house for many years and had lived year round for a time before I was born. My parents, who were never inclined to lazing around, noticed that there were many children in a neighboring community that were often on the streets and without food. As they began to inquire and talk to local pastors, they found that many of the children that they were seeing had one or both parents who were serving time in jail. Social services did not have adequate funds to help in this particular county. Many of our most affluent retirement and vacation communities have a visible population of people who are outside of the system and whose lives are in peril; places that some visitors consider paradise are often tragically broken and fraught with human need. On a temporary basis, my parents made tentative arrangements to cook one meal a week in a local congregation and invited a couple of friends to help them. Now, more than twenty years later, my mother, who is a widow and eighty-five, provides a weekly meal for upwards of sixty children. She is helped by a group of people from all denominations and walks of life. A local church donated a used van, so that the children can be picked up and brought home safely. A Roman Catholic charity provides grants and business people sometimes provide special meals—including oven-fresh pizza and fried chicken. At any given time you can find folks dropping off food to my mother, leaving non-perishables in her car while it is parked at church or at home. My mother makes jellies and jams and sells them in local farm stands to augment the cost of the food and other supplies that need to be purchased.

What was a simple act of noticing and inquiring has become a relationship of service that extends across a whole large community. It is impossible to go to a store without young children and older teens greeting Miss Betty. She and my Dad heard Jesus' invitation to Peter to feed the sheep—and they looked around. Often, if we will just look around and talk with others about the needs of the community, we can find a way to live out our faith and renew our communities. The joy and life that comes from a simple act of looking for God's call in familiar places, can transform individuals, families, and whole towns. And it can make it hard to take a quick trip to the grocery store!

In this chapter we will be focusing on ways to make it possible to make the story of Peter and Jesus our own story. You will be encouraged to find times and places where the community can gather as a whole to listen to God together as a family and to each hear their part in the larger story. The Sunday morning worship is one way to participate in the larger story of God's love for us. But there should be a variety of others ways to invite and include the whole family of God into the telling of the story. Peter had this discussion with Jesus because he wore his humanity on his sleeve; Peter was honest and hasty and often emotionally torn and confused. His love was real, as was his fear, but he wasn't afraid to risk it all to have a relationship with God. Jesus reminds us that we are welcomed and chosen into God's family, God's community, not because we always behave properly, but because we are loved, exactly as we are. Like Peter, we are chosen by God to care for the lambs, the sheep—the whole herd who follow Jesus. We all get to play the shepherd's part, lending our voices and gifts to the work of Christ on Earth, and in doing so, we all get to share in this wonderful work.

This chapter will help the leadership and people deepen their care and commitment for one another as they enliven their common lives. It involves education but not anything that feels like classroom drudgery. This will be a season of taking the lessons and insights from the exploring stage and turning them into a pattern of life in which everyone can participate—teaching and learning together.

Teaching

One of the critical ways that we act as Christ's disciples and feed the sheep, is to teach others and share the knowledge and experience we have gained. Although teaching is one of the basic building blocks of our common life, the ministry of teaching is one of the most overlooked and underutilized of ministries in our church today. We will focus on teaching when we have to, or when some kids show up and we want to keep them busy. Some of us will try to provide education for our children and young adults but we rarely consider how central teaching is to our common life. Jesus was first and foremost a teacher, a rabbi. In Matthew's gospel, a young man came to Jesus and called him "teacher," asking him what good must the young man do to have eternal life. Jesus suggested that the young man keep the Commandments, and when the young man replied that he had kept all of these, Jesus, the teacher, confronted him with the one thing he lacked—the ability to share the blessings he had received with others, especially those who had much less (Matthew 19:16–22).

If we are followers and disciples of Jesus, then we are meant to teach one another and participate in the constant education and nurture of our own faith and the faith of those around us. Our wealth, even the poorest and least among us, is in our experience and what we have learned from that experience. Jesus reminds us that our blessings of faith are riches that must be shared. Teaching others is one of simplest and most authentic ways in which we can share our blessings with others.

This call to teach is not for clergy alone, nor just for parents of young children, as is so often the expectation in many church communities. Teaching and learning are for every age and every walk of life, rich and poor alike. You might be saying to yourself, "What do I know that I could share with others?" Or you might be an individual who does not like public speaking or reading from scriptures to others. The traditional church models for teaching often limit our creative understanding of the ministry of teaching. When we say the word "teaching" in church, a vision of one prim parent with a gaggle of sticky, unruly, finger-painting children can come to mind. Or, even worse, we might imagine a dull adult forum where some enthusiastic person is sharing something utterly uninspired and uninspiring. But real teaching is much more organic to human beings than images like these suggest.

When we talk about teaching and education in general, we often are referring to the scholastic enterprise rather than the intuitive, interactive, and relational understanding of teaching, which all human are desirous of, and in which they are quite capable of participating. We teach the person sitting next to us about ourselves by the way we hold our body, through eye contact (or the lack thereof) and, most profoundly, through conversation, interaction, and touch. Parents teach their children most often through informal life lessons, by being observed modeling a positive (or dangerous) behavior. Adults in church communities teach the children most directly by their tone and interactions with young people—curious and interested or distanced and demeaning. We are all teachers by our actions; and I am suggesting that part of the way we grow a congregation together is to focus on teaching and learning—together.

A church, like other institutions in a particular community, has a responsibility to act as an educational institution. One of our primary roles is educational, albeit primarily religious and cultural. A leading educational scholar and professor of education at Harvard, Howard Gardner, writes, "Whatever their own cognitive and non-cognitive facets, educational institutions . . . ought to seek to inculcate in their students the highest degree of understanding. I embrace the position that educational institutions need to reach the broadest number of students, and that they must therefore be responsive to different forms of learning, performance and understanding." Gardner points out that having a broad understanding of education is best, and an even broader understanding of how many ways we learn is even more essential. Teaching, at its most basic level, is an invitation to understanding and the willingness to help another understand the complex nature of their environment. Effective teaching asks us to have the courage to remember what it was like to be without understanding, and the creativity to find ways to nurture and empower others to learn. The whole church family is called upon to be learners as well as teachers. A church community that is committed to growth should expect to learn in unfamiliar situations, and to teach in some nontraditional circumstances. Growth asks us to acknowledge that although what we think used to work, probably never worked for *everyone* anyway, so we all might as well try new ways of teaching and learning together. For a church community, that dynamic can be very threatening, but accepting that learning together can invite growth can also be a liberating experience for many people.

For a church family that wants to grow, teaching and learning will have to be considered in much more complex ways then has been done in years past. Each of us brings our personality and gifts to our lives together. But to reach understanding and to be able to teach and learn, we must attempt to define multiple ways of engaging in the educational process. Some of us learn best in very familiar, scholastic ways, through reading and repeating of concepts and ideas. Others of us must engage in a more hands-on process and must be guided and watched over as we manipulate the ideas and challenge them in concrete ways. And still others—we may need to sit at a distance, engaging with the visuals and intuitive ideas and textures that are part of the lesson. In any grouping of people, there will be several people who learn in each one of the three ways mentioned here—scholastic, apprentice, and intuitive. When considering any curriculum, and planning any event, I encourage you to take on several different ways of teaching (and learning) so that you are constantly expanding the circle of teachers and learners. By doing this, a small church can seem more welcoming to those who have found themselves as outsiders in other places.

The following questions are designed to encourage a discussion among the leadership of the church community about the teaching and learning that goes on in your midst. Ask yourself the following questions but do not be limited by their scope. Often an education committee will meet separately from the vestry and church leaders and will present a plan for church school and adult education without ever considering who is learning and who is teaching. The vestry and other leaders of the parish often avoid these conversations. Now is the season to embrace the idea that teaching and learning are critical to the growth and development of a community, and anything that you consider important must include the widest range of participants. This is not a time to put aside or defer answering the following questions, as they are so central to your continuing life together.

- Who does the majority of teaching in this church?

- Are these teachers scholastic, apprentice or intuitive?

- Or do they have a multiple approach?

- Are there skills and lessons that can be apprenticed in this congregation?

- Are there interpretive ways to tell the story of the people?

- Are there imaginative people who have a unique approach to their faith?

- Can they teach us something?

- Who is never asked to teach or considered to be a teacher?

- Is there something they can teach?

- What do we need to learn as a church family?

- Are there folks from the inside of our community that can teach us?

- Are there people from outside who can be invited to teach us, or companion with us?

- Is there anything that is keeping us from teaching and learning?

- Are there skills, practices that we need to learn?

- Are there skills and practices we can teach others?

Opportunity for Teaching and Learning

Once you have had a big discussion about the ministry of teaching in your church community, it is time to focus on one or two specific areas that can be taught and learned together. You will have amassed a huge variety of answers and opinions. Again, as in the previous chapter, there may well be an abundance of data. If you have more data and information than any one group can process, please don't be concerned for "more" in this case is a very good thing good thing. That abundance is a sign of a lively and growing church community, where each individual feels able to make a contribution. You are well on your way to finding growth and nurture in your midst. At this point, take some time to categorize the answers into the following four groups:

- Techniques and skills that can be taught now

- Concepts and ideas that can be taught now

- Techniques and skills that we need help with

- Concepts and ideas that we need help with

In this first cycle of church growth in this season, you will want to focus on the first two categories. The leadership can then take those first two, "right now" categories and implement an educational program for the whole church community. Let me give you some examples. How many in your congregation really know what the altar guild does? If you were to have several sessions, led by skilled and seasoned altar guild members, how much richer would your community be? If the one woman (or man) that always does outreach was to take everyone with her (him) over several weeks to the sites and people she (he) regularly interacts with, wouldn't your church family be richer and more experienced? Could you imagine having the entire parish know where the boiler is and how it is cared for, or the folks who organize hospitality and coffee hour teaching about their ministry?

Planning your late Pentecost or fall learning season with a focus on apprenticeship might well engage the largest group of learners and teachers, and would also invite those scholastic learners and teachers to find ways to integrate scripture and theology into the exercise of the teaching ministry. It might also elicit expressions of faith through visual arts as well as music, dance, and the like, by those who are inspired to express their learning through their art.

Cultural Teaching

One of the talents or expressed gifts that might arise out of the conversation about teaching could have to do with teaching about a particular culture or language group. Although to some, this kind of skill might be considered outside of what should be taught in a church setting, quite the opposite may well be true.

If we believe that God has created us, and that God considered all creation good, then there are way that our unique ethnic, racial, and language groups express their cultures as loving responses to a loving creator. We see God working through and in the midst of our unique cultural gifts and by sharing those gifts with other people, we demonstrate that a multitude of expressions are welcome in our communities of faith.

Several years ago, I had the opportunity to visit with a small, predominately Hawaiian parish on the north shore of Oahu. Like many small parishes, they struggled with growth and wanted to do more than just keep their doors open. They began to tap into the traditional wisdom of the elders in the church and began teaching hula and other traditional art forms to young people. There was some resistance to this idea for many of the older leaders in the community had been taught that their traditional sacred forms of expression were not allowed in the life of the church. They had been taught that to be Christian was to leave everything traditionally Native behind. Although that might seem an outdated idea to some, it has a prevailing undercurrent even now in many church communities. After several generations of being taught by word and example that all of your traditional approaches to God are considered heathen, it becomes very difficult to root out the lingering anxiety.

What this church community found was that there were a great number of young people and their parents who were hungry to learn about who they were. They wanted identity; they wanted belonging. They wanted to know about their people and their traditions so that they could understand in a fuller way their own creation and relationship to God. Folks who were not Hawaiian were also encouraged to learn alongside the native children, so that all could understand the people of the land and how God created them together. Through this process, they also expected that they would learn as a community how God still works through them in unique and marvelous ways.

Whatever cultural and local traditions exist in your church community, it is important to be very careful and sensitive in the process of inclusion within the life of a parish. I spoke earlier about the ways that some cultures were included in the life of the Christian church. There is much sensitivity around culture and language, and it is important to honor those feelings and concerns that arise, if you were to engage in a training program like the one the people took on in their small Hawaiian church. The clergy and leadership of a parish will do best to move slowly and carefully through this planning process, making sure to honor the traditions and identities of their diverse people, and honoring all basic ingredients to growth.

I want to share a story that I hope will be helpful at this point. When I was working on my doctoral research, I had the opportunity to stay at St. John's College in Auckland, New Zealand, and work with the Maori students and teachers who were there. I was there at the beginning of their fall semester (although it was February and early spring in my hemisphere) and they followed the custom of taking the whole school out to the local Marae* in order to be welcomed and taught by the people of the land. We spent several days together, sleeping in one large building and hearing their stories and traditions, so that we could know, as we studied together, where we were and who was welcoming us. It was a rich experience for me.

The last night we were at the Marae, we were invited to watch the dress rehearsal for the upcoming huka (traditional Maori dance) competition to be held in Auckland the following weekend. It was a rousing performance, men and women in traditional garb, tattooed, singing in incredible harmonies and performing a dance that included the women swinging poi (a traditional dish in Maori and Polynesian culture made of ground, baked, and fermented taro root) and the men pounding their chests. I was swept up by the experience. We sat watching, on a warm February evening, with unfamiliar constellations and stars swirling in the night sky above my head. I

---

*A Maori term which means the traditional meeting area of whanua or iwi, the focal point of the settlement consisting of the central area of a village, including its buildings and courtyards. Ryan, 1994, 37.

felt the firm reality of being a visitor from the other side of the planet. As I was watching and listening, trying to absorb everything, I started to notice that a tune sounded familiar. Because of my jet lag, and the newness of my surroundings, I initially ignored the sensation. But it was clearer and clearer to me that the Maori were singing and dancing to the tune of "Bridge Over Troubled Water" by Simon and Garfunkel. I chalked it up to jet lag and general confusion. The very next song, I was sure, was sung to the tune of Frank Sinatra's, "I Did It My Way." I was terrified that I was losing my mind. Here I was a doctoral student, doing research, a Native woman (Cherokee), and well trained in cultural anthropology. I should know better than to be taken by flights of fancy. I went to bed wondering whether I was having some sort of mental break. I kept my questions to myself.

Several days later, I was accompanying two young Maori college women who were showing me the city, their local Mhari, and taking me with them to witness their dancers preparing for the competition. I felt a little less foolish around these young people, and so finally, gathered up my courage and told them about my experience. They both started laughing. Finally one of the girls said to me, "That's so Maori!" And when I asked her to explain what she meant the other girl chimed in. "We like to find good things, steal them, and make them our own!" They both laughed and reassured me that I wasn't crazy and that all of the dancing groups used traditional words and set them to new tunes.

I tell this story as a reminder that all living cultures, and really all human beings, borrow and "steal" from one another. Whenever we are in contact with things (music, traditions, personal habits, etc.) that enrich our lives, we are bound to enfold them in our way of being. We are particularly challenged in the United States, where cultural contact and blending has happened over the centuries. I encourage you, through this story, to realize that all cultures make contact, interact, and use (and often share) what tools and insights they have. This is not to say that all culture is for the stealing, but that culture is a complex construct, varies from place to place, and is rich with meaning and insight. Judging a presentation for purity, then, can be a dangerous barrier. Inviting people to share what they have in the richness and complexity of their lives, invites an interaction that helps everyone develop, grow, and find a place in community.

People are drawn to communities where trust and honor abound. If someone has a concern about the planning, invite him or her to participate, and help that person to articulate their concerns in a safe environment. The time your community spends honoring those concerns will be an outward sign of true faithfulness and walking with Christ.

There are multiple ways to teach about culture and identity. Dance and music are among them, but cooking and traditional crafts can also be valuable teaching resources. Some parishes that want to grow set aside a time when everyone can learn together, even if there are many small groups and a diversity of skills and concepts being taught. One parish I worked with did their Christian education as a Sunday evening activity, once a month. They put a simple supper together, which was prepared by some members of the church community. If anyone wanted to learn how to make the traditional dishes they were preparing, they could come early and learn, while helping out at the same time. After the meal, several different multi-age groups formed to do Bible study, study language, create a craft, play an instrument or sing, or participate in a storytelling workshop. There was always an abundance of laughter, food, coffee, and conversation. Various people volunteered to act as teachers for one time with a particular group, but everyone expected to learn together. There was not a huge time commitment, but everyone found an activity that brought them some meaning and deepened their relationships with others in the community.

We began this book by talking about the importance of identity and belonging, and I am bringing it up again because these elements are so critical to any program of church growth. The critical need in planning your education programs is to have identity development and belonging (deepening of relationships) as central to your design. I believe that the simplest programs, particularly in the first season, work best. To grow, you do not have to tackle everything at once, or have a program that looks like the church down the street. Design your programs with identity and belonging in mind and develop from there a course of action. And always remember to feed people and care for their persons with adequate food, breaks, and gentle expectations.

Attention to Ritual

At the end of any educational process, it is essential that you have a time or space for reflection. Some folks like to have a formal service at the end of their educational programs, such as Compline, Evening Prayer, or a simple Eucharist. A rotating group of learners might want to be responsible for designing a small service of worship and reflection that is not from the Prayer Book and might want to explore other worship resources. The Church Publishing website has links to several incredible resources that provide innovative and timely resources, many of them free of charge. One of those resources is www.theworshipwell.org, and there are many others that can be helpful resources for your reflection and worship time. This group might also want to look at the ideas and skills that were shared in the sessions that have just concluded and help everyone reflect on what they have learned together. Often, it is best not to leave this planning to the clergy, but it might be, for instance, an exercise for the artists and musicians in the group. This is not to say that many clergy people are not gifted and artistic. But using the special talents of people in the group may help create a richer mix in the common life of a faith community.

One simple way to incorporate the cultural learnings that have happened is to find a simple and familiar part of the worship service that is (or can be) translated into the various languages and/or customs of your community. My friend Bishop Mike Smith of North Dakota often asks people to sing the doxology in their own language. He asks people to sing, in turn, and then everyone sings it together in English. This is a simple but powerful way to demonstrate the breadth of God's gifts across a community. Often people try to translate large parts of the service and formalize the language and customs. Whenever there is a need for a community to grow and stretch, it is always best to introduce new things in the simplest and gentlest of ways. You might not have people who can translate and sing the doxology, but maybe they could translate the words of the peace. Maybe someone could translate something as familiar as, "the Lord be with you," and its reply, "and also with you." Try in as many ways as possible to let people hear and see their language (and other gifts) as an integral part of the worship life of your church community. Simple things can make all the difference in the world for someone who has felt like an outsider and unwelcome for a long time.

Filling the Well

Jesus met the woman at the well. We don't know all the details about her, but we know she was a Samaritan woman, and that Jesus told her everything she'd ever done. (John 4:1–42)

Despite knowing her dreadful failings, despite the fact that her people were considered outsiders and unwanted in the Jewish community, he asked her for water, he talked with her, he spent time with her and by doing so, changed her life. Jesus reached out to the woman, and because of her testimony, her story told over and over again, many others came to know him and believe in him. This story reminds us that our faith is most often transmitted in the simplest of encounters, not from the pulpit or through any curriculum. Jesus sat with this woman, and she sat with Jesus. A deep well was in their midst and although the well that was their common focal point was full of water, the well we need to fill is the living well. Our lives of faith need deep wells filled with hope, compassion, support, and resilience. The artificial boundaries that we set up between cultures and people are solidified and institutionalized when our wells are empty. Growing a faith community requires us to have deep wells, overflowing with mercy, generosity, and courage. Folks are drawn to communities where their lives can be transformed and renewed. We need to have deep, full wells of living water, the kind of water that Jesus was telling the woman about.

How do we fill the well? It is simpler then we sometimes think. Filling the well requires us to be in relationship together and to commit to doing the critical work of encouraging and empowering one another. We have already said that education is something a community can engage in together. Filling the well, so that everyone is enriched and growing is essential to our growth. Mentoring and companioning are two of the best ways to fill our wells to overflowing and to encourage one another as we grow together.

Mentors

In the business world, mentors are frequently seasoned professionals who take an interest in the careers of younger persons. These mentors often act as coaches for those who are just starting out, teaching techniques and skills, and helping them move on when discouraging crises happen. Some young people have experience with organizations like Big Brother and Big Sister and have positive outcomes from having a mentor in their growing years. Some colleges and universities have peer mentors for students so that newer students have a support system to navigate through their first years of study. From all walks of life, people in your community have experience with, or as a mentor. Almost everyone that has ever served as a mentor describes it as a rich and rewarding experience. The mentor often believes that they are getting more out of the relationship than the one being mentored. Those who have been mentored talk about how that one person alone profoundly changed their life. Someone took time to sit and listen. Someone took time to help them turn around when they stumbled, were in trouble, or were simply overwhelmed. The mentor was a deep well for the one being mentored and very often that person turned around and mentored other young people. Mentoring is a contagious, life-giving activity.

When we talked about mentoring in a church community, we knew that there were people with gifts and skills that also have some time to share with a younger person. One need not set up a highly structured mentor program to have success and growth with mentor relationships. You might begin with taking several months, or a liturgical season, and ask older folks to act as mentors to the community's young people. The simplest assignments are the easiest to follow, so maybe the mentors could be directed to spend an hour (more is fine) with the young person and have several meals during that time period. The initial attempt to establish a mentoring relationship should provide lots of flexibility and always the opportunity to move out of relationships that aren't working. Mentoring should not be limited to exclusively younger and older folks, but could be a new and long-time member relationship, new parent with a seasoned parent, etc. The idea is to provide support for those who are testing out their wings of faith and to be a deep well for others as they deepen their relationship with God. Time after time, mentoring also proves to fill the well of the mentor.

Companions

In the church we often use the term "companions" when we are talking about ministry with seniors. In a typical setting, someone volunteers to spend time with an elder who is a shut-in or confined to a nursing home. This person might read their friend a story, do some shopping, or simply provide companionship for a lonely older person. I would like to expand this concept and suggest that despite our busy lives in contemporary society, many people of all ages describe their biggest personal challenge as isolation or loneliness. Very busy people, who are surrounded by people in their work or home settings, often still feel isolated and without a grounded sense of belonging. Companions can help in the process of growing a church community. A simple program of offering companionship for study, recreation, learning, or simple chores can encourage others to see your church community as a place that provides a needed response to modern isolation.

A companions program can be basic. Choose a few areas of concern to begin with, areas in which someone in your church can provide some skills (or equipment, like a car) and to which others might be invited to join. They should be simple activities—for instance, gardening, cooking, bowling, grocery shopping, or meals out. I encourage you to consider this as an intergenerational program, which provides friendship and support for people in your community. Providing safe relationships for people across the breadth of your community develops a deep well of understanding and a network of communication and support that will draw others to your faith community.

Young people can be encouraged to teach through a companion program. Our young people have incredible skills that they can share; skills which come easily to young people might be a struggle for an older person. I am not talking about yard work, or heavy lifting, since too many churches expect young people to take on menial tasks. I am talking about the unique language and skills that our youth have in simple technology. What more mature adults may struggle with, young people under twenty-five can tackle while they are engaged in doing several other things. I worked with a youth group once that offered their time reprogramming elders' VCRs, DVD players, phones, computers, etc. They did they simple tasks that they take for granted but which can flummox older adults. Creative skill and gift identification allows the companion process to be more than a transaction—what one person can do for another—it can build a community of believers who help encourage and identify the unique gifts that can be hidden in plain sight. Most youth don't know how their elders struggle with very simple technology since some of us were raised without that language. Find a way to make bridges between people in you church community and you will give your community strong relationships with deep roots that will strengthen and enhance the larger population.

I would suggest that you come up with a name for this program that reflects the values and/or needs of your community. This program isn't meant to suggest a dating service, but a way for people to move out of the closed circles that have isolated them and into the larger community of faith, reaching across age, culture, and other barriers that normally occur in our churches. Young people can take the lead in naming programs and creating art and interactive media that can help explain what your church is trying to accomplish. Many people who are seeking out a church community will look for initial information on the web. They will be enticed or click by, depending on how accessible and attractive your website is. And if you do not have a website, this is the time to seek out individuals in your community who can create one for you. This could be part of your companion program—teaching others how to put a website together and how to maintain it once it is launched.

The goal of having mentors and companions is to fill the well with the most potent, life-giving force there is—love; not "squishy" romantic love, but the love that is fostered in the day-to-day, side-by-side notion of a community working and worshipping together. There is no more powerful force for growth than real love, which takes people right where and as they are and calls them friend. The love that Jesus had for the woman at the well was made evident in his truth telling and willingness to share of himself with her. He did not walk away because she was different or had made some mistakes. He took her at face valued and affirmed her. He crossed barriers of culture, gender, and age, and invited her into a relationship that would change her life. Every time we take the chance to engage another, we are risking change. We will be changed by other people and they will be changed by us. Growth is at the center of all of this, so if you are willing to be made uncomfortable for a period or season, then God's love can work in the midst of the change, bridging all sorts of distances.

God's love places ultimate value on people and our relationship with others. We find God in the midst of our relationships, not far away from people and their daily lives. Mentors and companions are critical to the life of a church as it grows. They are those who are willing to walk, share, listen, and live with others as they grow in faith. They are the people who have been fed by the nurturing and care of others, and who can't help but give others the same kind of support and care. It's contagious, and simple at the same time. If you can find people who are willing to take time with others, share tasks, and give back to the community, then your church is poised and sturdy enough to grow. This is how we fill the well, with people reaching out to others, valuing and sharing with another. The experience of reaching out sets in motion an endless series of events, which make the whole community richer and stronger.

Weaving

The next phase of this season of nurturing the people and filling the well, is a period where there is a specific focus on the leadership of the church community. What attributes and behaviors might the leaders adopt that can help their parish or church community grow? How can they be leaders in their unique community in an authentic way that is not borrowed from other communities, but organic to their own? The leadership of any community, I believe, has the most impact when it is able to understand the story of the people and to articulate that story within the framework of the story of the larger church community. This is simply weaving. Weaving is the activity in which leaders help others tell their story and find a voice within the whole community. They are weaving the individual into the bigger story of the church family, grafting the single into the whole in a way that is life-giving and empowering.

The research in cognitive development done by Howard Gardner and others at Harvard University School of Education, can lend some insight into the importance of the activity of **weaving** by church leadership. Howard Gardner has done extensive study on the cognitive elements of successful leaders in unique communities. He writes that, " the ultimate impact of any given leader depends most significantly on the particular story that he or she relates or embodies and the reception to that story on the part of audiences (or collaborators or followers) (1995:14). Gardner believes that "story"—the narrative of the people—is the vehicle through which communities identify within themselves and the way in which leaders voice the collective identity of the people. Story as both identity and embodiment are central to understanding Gardner's concept of leadership within community. If a leader is able to verbalize the collective story and assign roles to both leaders and followers within that story, then the community is able to support and affirm the authority and authenticity of the leader.

Gardner chooses to focus on the cognitive (higher order values and goals) inspired by these leaders in order to understand the outcomes (impacts) on direct relations with followers. As stated earlier, leadership within the church demands personal integration and a strong identity (both personal and collective). Gardner reminds us that an authentic leader must embody and participate in the story of the people.

In my own cultural community (Cherokee/Native American) this story and the ability to weave stories together, has special significance as many of our personal and collective (tribal) identities are formed through a storytelling process. The "story" of the people and an individual is essential to healthy Native identity formation. Howard Gardner's unique approach to leadership has been developed over years as he has studied the ways in which people learn. Gardner suggests that there are multiple models for acquiring knowledge, and that many people's learning styles are directly correlated to their culture of origin. Gardner's body of research on "multiple intelligences," or the multiple modes of learning acquisition and development, has had an enormous impact on the present theories of education and has challenged the field to explore the intellectual disposition of the learner in order to develop an integrated approach to teaching (1995). Cognitive leadership development, "designs vehicles that simultaneously help to uncover and foster an individual's competences" (1995:16). Gardner suggests that personal and societal aspects of leadership are interrelated, and he writes, "Our society has tended to ignore the impact of interpersonal experiences in part because it is not readily abstracted and measured when analyzing differences in competences and achievement" (1993:61).

We talked earlier in this chapter about the importance of multiple approaches to learning and teaching. We explored some of the possible programs that a church community might provide to encourage and grow their local church community. By focusing on the practice of the church leadership, I am suggesting that since relationships are so critical to the life of the parish or congregation, each person in a leadership position should be encouraged to stretch themselves and learn how to tell their personal story in light of the story of the whole community. This might happen in the context of a dinner, or an evening gathering, where church leaders took turns telling about how they came to be part of the life of your church. Or, there might be an informal time, during coffee hour for example that is dedicated to hearing one of your leaders' stories. Your leaders might want to write articles for the church newsletter or website, if you have one. There are multiple ways to learn and teach—and likewise, there are multiple ways to tell your story. There might be a person among your leadership who likes to take photographs, or present a story in some other medium. Encourage it! Someone who is listening will light up because he or she discovers that one of the present leaders thinks as they do and expresses themselves in a similar fashion. The whole exercise is designed to make connections between people, connections that can continue and be deepened.

Over the past months, particularly if you have taken seriously the work of exploring and mapping described in Chapter Three, you will have realized that the identity of a church community is formed in part by people who are actually outsiders to the community. The leadership and people of the church have spent time with others from across the broader community and in partnered churches to learn about your own parish. Part of the work of this season is to weave the stories and perceptions, the ones that used to be alien or unarticulated, into the whole story of your church community. Part of the weaving process encourages taking the contrasting colors, ideas, and perceptions, and adding them to the fabric, the story—to the identity of the people. Your leadership and members might want to review some of the things you have learned about other people's perceptions of you, and bind their insights into your mission statement, or into other tools for growth. This might also be an opportune time to invite folks that you worked with in Chapter Three to share a meal, or speak to your community at a worship service or a congregational function. Telling the story invites adaptation and deeper understanding. Sharing the story can also provide points of inclusion for those who might not have felt welcome before. Weaving your story together with the story of the larger community can make some people uncomfortable. Your strand becomes woven in with, and may contrast with other strands of the whole cloth. But we grow by stretching and bending, not by folding in on ourselves and being an exclusive strand of God's story of love for all.

Any way you can tell the story of a loving community that has grafted an outsider and transformed them into insiders will be productive and encouraging to all. Weaving is the art of taking separate strands and dancing them together, one over the other, behind and beside, until a blanket or tapestry is woven and a beautiful piece of artwork, clothing, or warmth has been created. No one strand is lost, but rather, is articulated more clearly next to another. In music, the beauty of harmony is in the whole chord, the dark and light tones and the bright and shining notes in between. Like chords or fabric, our weaving is a strengthening of the whole community.

Stewardship

At this stage of the church year, if you are using this chapter during late Pentecost, serious discussions are probably underway about the budget for the upcoming year. If you are like every other congregation I have worked with, people are getting anxious about pledges and money to fund all of the ministries and events that the church wants to make available. Many parishes struggle, beg, plead. and wring their hands about income and rarely will someone willingly volunteer to head the stewardship campaign. Episcopalians are particularly loath to talk about money, and although some take great pride in our ability to reflect and have conversation about many, many controversial subjects, when it gets to money, we are mute. I believe we struggle so much because money is tied to many people's individual identities and we are yet to be a people who know our corporate or communal identity. We, as a church, are often like adolescents, hoarding the little we have because we are so afraid of being vulnerable and without. Many have not moved to a place where they see every-thing they have, and everything they are as a gift from God.

When individuals feel secure and alive in a congregation, they are often very generous. They give, not out of obligation, but because they are grateful and want others to experience what they have experienced. When individuals are grateful and generous, congregation thrive and grow. If individuals see them-selves embraced as part of a larger family, the whole community is enriched and deepened. Our struggle with stewardship is often an indication that our people do not see themselves and their gifts as essential fabric in the life of the church. Steward-ship and giving are much less of a struggle when there is a sense of interdependency and connectivity in the life of the parish or congregation—a integrated, complex, and dynamic relationship of people to one another, and, together, with God.

So how can we think about and practice stewardship in an integrative and holistic way that encourages people to take on the risk of generosity and vulnerability? First, we must realize that God designed us from the beginning and invites us to con-tinue to live as stewards—caretakers of what we have been given. When we are truly living into stewardship together, we are acknowledging our dependence on God (we didn't get here on our own), our dependence on one another (I can't do this on my own), and the community's dependence on our gifts (we must share what we have been given). This is scary stuff, and most Episcopalians, and I daresay most Americans, truly want to believe that we are self-made and it is through our own per-sonal effort that we have what we have. Living stewardship makes a shift towards understanding life as a gift we cannot control—the only thing we can do is share it.

Practicing and planning for stewardship in your congregation might focus then on the gifts you have received and on proclaiming God's generosity in your midst. What gifts do you have that inform who you are as a community?

In one parish I served outside of Philadelphia, the organ died on Christmas. Although it was a painful process of loss, and it could not be rebuilt and was finally replaced with an electronic organ, the gift of lively music, and how people adapted and offered their musical gifts in the interim was so astounding, that the entire community recognized a tremendous blessing. Someone had the brilliant idea to make the old organ keys into ornaments and key chains. Each person who participated in the stewardship of the congregation got a memento of the organ. Music was the lifeblood of this parish and the entire community (children included) had lived through a profoundly challenging time and had seen new blessings and abundance in the midst of it. So everyone proudly took a piece of what had been and gave generously to what was to be—so that everyone could thrive and understand God's abundance.

I serve presently as bishop-in-residence to a church in Jersey City, New Jersey. This community has tripled in size over the past five years and is one of the most racially diverse and youthful congregations in the region. Stewardship can be particularly challenging in a young, diverse, growing congregation for the simple fact that many young families have very limited (and/or completely committed) incomes. And many people come from very different religious experiences, or are coming to church for the first time in years. This parish is also blessed with many creative and artistic folks. One quite renowned artist designed the logo of the church, which depicts the beauty of the church along with the diversity of the people both entering the church and already sitting in the pews. The new logo, a true gift, really captured the sense of the church community. As part of the stewardship campaign, the logo was enlarged and reinforced and then cut up into jigsaw puzzle pieces. Each week, more puzzle pieces were put into place as people pledge their income, their effort, and their talent to the church community.

Stewardship can be something other than a painful and necessary exercise. It can be a moment of highlighting the gifts of the community and celebrating the abundance that God has provided and continue to provide for the future ministries of our communities. It is an opportunity to weave the lives of people together, to tell the stories of blessings and gifts and to invite others to share in the life of your particular faith community. Your church is a gift, and stewardship, at its best, is a celebration of the gifts in your midst.

A reminder before we move on to the notion of sanctuary—whatever weaving we are doing—is *integrative* work. Integrative work is both a developmental and an educational process. We need to be mindful that people learn in many ways, most often in non-structured academic settings. Whatever goals and mission foci you may have set for your congregation, make sure that these aspirations are reflected in the church school and adult education programs. Whatever aspects of culture and identity have been highlighted and emphasized in other settings should be carried over into any ongoing educational programs. Many communities find this challenging, when in reality it is quite simple. If you are very few in number, you are likely having intergenerational learning situations anyway.

This is an opportunity to identify what is important to your church community and have it visible in every possible way, in every situation. For example, ask yourselves, what do our walls say? Are there signs pointing to what we are truly about? Is this season of weaving and sanctuary obvious to everyone? At the close of late Pentecost, if you are using this chapter in that season, are you ready to move on to Advent, certain that everyone has been involved in the process of being nurtured and filling the well? To move on without a large number of people on board can be dangerous. Those who might want to join your congregation, might not know how to do that if a majority of your people are unaware of what you have been doing over the past months. Make sure the newsletter, your signs, your website (if you have one) and every other vehicle is used to share what you are doing with the whole community. If you do not have a website, now is the time to invest the time and money into creating one. Often, there is someone in your church community with the skills and the time to make this happen for very little cost. Many dioceses can provide web services and often have a committee of volunteers who will share their time and know how. Don't be shy to ask for help because this season of learning and teaching is ripe for everyone to learn something new. You just have to ask, out loud, and the process will start.

Sanctuary

From the prophet Isaiah, we hear these wonderful, comforting words about the community of God as envisioned as the kingdom of heaven:

> For as the rain and snow come down from heaven, and do not return until they have watered the earth, making it bring forth and sprout, giving seed to the sower and bread to the eater, so shall my word be that goes out from my mouth; it shall not return to me empty, but it shall accomplish that which I purpose, and succeed in the thing for which I sent it. For you shall go out in joy, and shall be led back in peace; the mountains and hills before you shall burst into song, and all the trees of the field shall clap their hands. (Isaiah 55:10–12 NRSV)

We all hope that our local church community provides some measure of this sense of sanctuary, the closeness of God's abundance and the courage to provide safe haven for all. Many times, our church family, particularly when we are small and overburdened—financially, programmatically, or in a host of other ways—we tend to take personally the natural and expected failures that occur in the course of trying to grow a congregation. Many congregations will have great programs, work hard at including newcomers, and then blame the priest, pastor, or church-school teacher when a small disaster happens. We are often our most critical over the smallest of errors. We are often critical and embarrassed because we tried something new and it was minimally awkward or, in the extreme, a complete disaster. We then look for someone to blame instead of honoring the fact that doing new things is in the act itself, awkward. Transitions are challenging. Ask any teenager and they will confirm that rapid growth and change is terrifying and makes you feel very awkward. We often want to act out toward others rather than say out loud how awkward and uncomfortable we truly feel. The role of the leadership is to help people articulate these terrors in a safe and supportive way.

Sanctuary for all requires that the leadership of the church community be particularly vigilant that this church is a safe place for all. That includes the clergy as well as the lay leaders, the children, the seniors as well as the choir. God's vision of community from Isaiah is a place of peace, where people come and go with joy surrounding them. God's vision does not include living with the threat of terror from without or within. Our experience of daily life in the parish can be very far from that. Remember that folks are coming into the community hoping, praying, aching, desiring to experience some measure of that sanctuary, that peaceful meadow of God's vision. None of us has it alone, but it is something we can model and share with one another. We can make our church a safe and welcome place, a sanctuary, even when we are angry or disappointed. No program can thrive, no matter how well devised and implemented, if there is a sense of danger and hostility lurking around the edges of every meeting or gathering.

The leadership of the parish has a special responsibility to observe and restore situations and relationships that have become hostile. Often, along with the priest or pastor, if a troubled individual or difficult situation is confronted early, it can be simple to resolve the surrounding problems. If a situation has been allowed to fester, it can swallow up every good thing that has ever been accomplished. Sanctuary is necessary for our personal and collective survival. If this is a struggle for your particular situation, there are resources available from dioceses and the national church, as well as through Quaker, Methodist, and other groups that focus on mediation, peace initiatives, and other interpersonal trainings that can help you create a safe environment for all. And please don't be discouraged. When-ever human beings are in close proximity, there is conflict. Con-flict is part of relationship, since we all have such different approaches to experience, teaching, learning, and leading. The sooner you are able to identify the conflicts in your community, the sooner a solution and rich experiences of working together for the health of all can be witnessed.

The notion of sanctuary also invites us to provide space for quiet reflection and healing. As a community grows, there is more noise and busy-ness, more opportunities for relationships and with that, more possibilities of conflicts. Good people hurt each other because they are trying their best and still are human. Christian communities are as susceptible to conflict and likely to clash as any other human organism. Be ready to forgive one another and actively seek each other's forgiveness when hurts or conflicts appear. Recognizing that conflict is part of growth, a real and necessary part of new life, will ease the burden for all. Articulating the reality that conflict is a natural occurrence, particularly in growth times, allows everyone to move from blame to forgiveness. Raising awareness about con-flict is one thing, but what you do with it as a community is another thing entirely. The one thing I know for sure is that con-flict will not go away on its own. Take time to plan events and have trained people to respond to the conflicts that arise between people, and within people. Some parishes chose this time to add a regularly scheduled service of healing. If you have not added a prayer or healing service to your rota, now is an excellent time to do so. Other parishes build, borrow, or invite spiritual exercises, like a labyrinth, or a silent retreat into their schedules. Others find expressive events, like a memorial serv-ice for those lost in the war, a 9/11 memorial, or the like, to help them deal with their external and internal conflicts. Whatever you do, make sure to recognize the frailty of the human condi-tion, honor one another in every way possible, and plan for events and speakers that can help a variety of people deal with the relationships and events that are tearing them away from knowing safety in God and in community.

Sundays

You may, by now, be annoyed with me for reminding you to ask yourselves about Sundays and the space and time issues that have been with us from the beginning. This is really such an important part of understanding your community and the growth you are called to that I am willing to be an irritant for the gospel. Do people outside the church building have any idea what is going on there? The people inside your community probably have a better idea what goes on than they did in the past, but please don't forget to ask simple questions about what else could be going on, and who else might need to share your space and time. The hardest part of church growth is not the programming, but the realization that this is an ongoing, eternal stretching. There is no moment when you get to sit down and say, "We're fine, just as we are." God will always find some person or situation to send your way that will change the dynamic within your church community and will challenge the relationships in your midst. Committing yourselves to the sensitive care of others means you will have to keep your eyes and ears open and respond to the answers as they come. It is hard work, but along with challenges God always doubles and triples the consequent blessings.

Another critical aspect of Sunday mornings is the ability of the liturgy and the preacher to weave the story of the people into the story of God. Folks coming for the first time need to know that the gospel has practical applications in your community. Whoever is preaching is reminded to share from the heart. An authentic story about how the gospel speaks to you is the most powerful thing you can share. Some clergy might have to set aside their reliance on their preaching classes from seminary and pay closer attention to what is happening in the community. Many times there are rich stories of God acting in our midst, if we are willing to be genuine, vulnerable, and authentic, rather than careful and perfect. I want to be clear that I am not suggesting that we should cross lines of propriety when preaching or delve into psychotherapeutic jargon. Rather, we are all called to make the gospel come alive in our lives, right where we are, and our own stories of our struggles and insights can be true gifts for the entire community.

Years ago, it was Easter season, and I was preparing to preach on John 10:11–16. Jesus said, "I am the good shepherd. The good shepherd lays down his life for his sheep. . . . I have other sheep who do not belong to this fold. I must bring them also, and they will listen to my voice." I was imagining rich pastoral images, a hillside covered with sheep, and preparing to bring support and comfort to my congregation by painting a pretty picture for them. I thought I was writing a very powerful sermon when the phone rang. It was a neighbor of Paula, the church secretary. The neighbor was distraught because Paula's cows had gotten out, it was Friday, and the traffic to the beach was picking up, and the cows were headed for the highway. Paula was nowhere to be found, probably out doing errands for her family. I volunteered to come help and enlisted the aid of the sexton, Otis. Off we went, an early spring day, with a little cold rain drizzling down to challenge visibility and comfort.

When we spotted the cows they were in an adjacent field, about a quarter mile from home, but just a hundred yards from the highway. I gave it my best, trying to corral these four animals. Every time I had them headed in the right direction, they pivoted and headed back to the highway. I had no idea what to do. Otis was whistling and flapping his arms. Obviously, we had no experience, but we were trying. The neighbor finally brought out her ATV, and tried to round the cows up with that. She circled them, trying to move them from the highway and it would work—but only temporarily. We were wet, cold, and feeling both frustrated and frightened. More than an hour passed and we were worn down. The neighbors' children were tired, hungry for lunch, and on the verge of crying inconsolably. As things were at their worst, Paula pulled down the long driveway to her small farm. She looked at all of us and wondered what we were doing. Her response was something like, "Oh, for heaven's sake!" She then opened the gate, and whistled and these four sweet, contrite cows proceeded to make a beeline for the open gate. Within a few minutes they were safely locked inside. Her cows knew her voice and knew that she was in charge.

I had to rewrite my sermon that day, and I have had to rewrite many since that time. It was most powerful for me to tell people the story of the cows, and my inability to make any change for the good. The three of us trying to be cowherds that day, had to rely on the one whose voice they knew, the one who was in charge. Like the cows, I often want to go my own way, but God's activity is always about opening the gate, and calling us home and feeding us.

Find stories of yourself and the people you serve with. And let stories find you. If you are willing to be vulnerable and demonstrate God's activity in your life, and your need for God, then many who come in will stay. Those who stay will want to weave their story with the stories you tell. They will want to be woven in to the gospel with the whole community.

EXERCISES

1. **Scavenger hunt:** From the exploration part of this chapter, find a list of twenty locations, stores, oddities, strange signs on buildings, works of art, interesting people, etc., that you have discovered in the process. Make up teams (intergenerational is best with each team having a designated driver) and give each team a list of those twenty items that have been discovered. Give them a certain time; depending on your geography, this could take several hours or a whole afternoon. They need to not only find the item, but also collect something from that person, place, or thing designated. This means they will have to tell people what they are doing and ask for something like a signature, napkin, or the like. Use your imaginations with what people bring back—maybe they will make a collage or poster together—but make sure they interact with the community. At the end, an ice cream party, piñata, or other festive fellowship time should be planned with crazy or silly prizes for everyone (i.e., for the team who got lost the most, the team who was first, last, and most confused).

2. **Treasure Chest:** An old chest is best, but a box with a lid painted to look like a treasure chest is fine. Many toy or party stores will have something to use for this. Fill the box with large colored index cards. Each card should have the name of a member of the church community on it. There should be plenty extra for visitors and occasional members. Leave the box by the main door of the sanctuary. Encourage everyone to pick out a card (with someone else's name on it) and find out all sorts of things about this person when interviewing them. The cards can be decorated, pictures added or drawn, and find any expressive way this person can be honored and encouraged for who they are. When a card is full, return it to the box until all the cards are full (or by a set date). Then take turns reading the cards out loud at announcement times. A wide variety of people can read these out loud to everyone, or you might want to ask the person who interviewed the "treasured person" to read it. Some or all of the cards could be copied into your newsletter.

CHAPTER FIVE

A New People of God
Strangers No More and Renaming Home

(Can be used during Advent)

The word that Isaiah son of Amoz saw concerning Judah and Jerusalem. In the days to come the mountain of the Lord's house shall be established as the highest of the mountains, and shall be raised above the hills; all nations shall stream to it. Many people shall come and say, "Come let us go up to the mountain of the Lord, to the house of the God of Jacob: that God may teach us his ways and that we may walk in his paths." For out of Zion shall go forth instruction, and the word of the Lord from Jerusalem. He shall judge between nations, shall arbitrate for many peoples; they shall beat their swords into plowshares, and their spears into pruning hooks; nation shall not lift up sword against nation, neither shall they learn war any more. O house of Jacob, come, let us walk in the light of the Lord! (Isaiah 2:1–5)

This reading, for the first Sunday of Advent, Year A, reminds us that the new community that God is making within us and around us, is nothing less than a vision of the heart of God. Over the past weeks and months, as your faithful community has been working to grow in love and service, you have also been expanding your insights into God's call to grow and encompass a larger body of people and to reach beyond the normal boundaries of nations. The words of Isaiah are often found to be a comfort, this clear picture of swords beaten into plowshares and the promise of a gathering of nations without the devastation of war and conflict. This vision of God transforming our aggression and hurt into the tools of abundance and transformation seem both hopeful—and impossible.

We know that when two or three are gathered, Christ promises to be in the midst of us. We also know that when two or three human beings are gathered together, there will be conflict. It is to this dichotomy that we are called, and it is here that we find our true nature and community. We are simultaneously creatures of habit and history, as well as people of new vision and transformation. We live continually in the "once upon a time" and the "not yet." Here we are in the pregnant reality of new life on the horizon with the anxiety of incompleteness and struggle.

It seems appropriate then, to consider Advent the time of becoming. This time of renaming and being transformed can be both exciting and terrifying, and it can challenge even those most committed to the idea of growth. This is the season where we will put all of the previous work into action and hand over some of the responsibility of the community to those who have recently joined with us, or those who have taken a renewed interest in the life of the parish. If you and your community are having moments of anxiety and apprehension at this point, let me reassure you, your feelings are authentic and true and appropriate to this season. This whole process of congregational development, if we take it seriously, demands that every member of the community stretch and grow. It expects that some rather alien and strange people and customs might come into our midst and become part of our family. Since most Episcopal churches are family-size congregations (eighty or fewer on Sunday mornings), by committing to church growth, we are planning on having our family change both its look and its nature. For many of us that can be a frightening thought, and it is also, at this moment, that many programs of church growth come to a grinding halt.

I would like to share a story that I hope will illuminate the present concerns. When I was a rector in Delaware, every year, like many churches, we struggled with the timing of the Christmas pageant. When I arrived, the church held to the traditional custom of holding the pageant on Christmas Eve, during the late afternoon family service. The event was stressful for everyone, as rehearsals usually happened after church on Sundays and people were rushed. Then, on Christmas Eve, the children and their parents were at wits end, swirling in all the still incomplete preparations for their family Christmas. We had a faithful pageant director, who tried to hold everyone together. We often joked about the similarities to the *Best Christmas Pageant Ever* by Barbara Robinson, first published in 1972, the story of the wild Herdman children who overrun a normally tranquil Christmas pageant event. The disasters and anxieties were very real to us. We finally, with the help of the liturgy committee and the vestry, changed the timing of the Christmas pageant, so that it fell during the Sunday service on the last Sunday in Advent. The children took part in the Sunday service, as well as presenting the pageant. For a season or so, this arrangement worked out well. Then, just when we thought we had a really successful formula, the pageant director decided to retire.

As rector, I began asking who would be willing to direct the pageant for the coming year. People were polite but emphatic that they were too busy, but otherwise would love to help. Even parents who wanted their children to have starring roles could not be persuaded to be pageant director. I was faced with the worst dilemma. Direct the pageant myself or, horrors, do without the pageant all together. Everyone wanted the pageant and stated that it was central to our life as a parish. When everything looked bleak, my eldest daughter made an offer. She had just graduated from college with a degree in theatre and was living back at home. "I'll direct the pageant," she said. "I'll direct it, if you will let me rewrite it." Panic set in. Here I was, with a willing and able person, who was qualified and talented in directing young people. But I was going to have to let go of the traditional script that we had used, and let her take control of it. She was young and edgy. After some deep breathing, I agreed—she could do it.

In a private moment in my office, shortly after I had said yes, I was filled with fear and remorse. I started praying, not knowing what else to do. Throughout Advent, I was not allowed to interfere with what she was doing and she asked that I not try to rewrite the script. Doom and panic washed over me on a regular basis during Advent and I knew that these loving people would find a way to get rid of me after the disaster that would surely happen.

When I finally saw the dress rehearsal, I was amazed. The pageant opened with one of the children, who was acting the part of pageant director, inquiring where all the children were. The doors of the church burst open and a dozen little girls burst in, all loudly demanding to be Mary. They argued among themselves about who was the prettiest, etc., until the director quieted them all down. She asked where the boys were. Young boys started appearing from under pews and from behind the pulpit and lectern. They told her that they don't like the pageant because they have to wear smelly bathrobes and never get to say anything. The director promises to do something about that, and everyone exits. One of the children reappears, climbs into the pulpit, and acts as narrator. The narrator tells the people that the story of the first Christmas tells us that God is in the midst of us and that we are all part of the family of God. We all have a part.

And as the pageant unfolded, I was astounded by the richness of the nativity story. Some of the toughest young boys played angels, and the very loudest and toughest among them played the archangel Gabriel. Several of the girls were innkeepers. There were both girls and boys acting as shepherds. The best part was that the girls and boys all rotated the roles of Mary and Joseph in the costumes they had also worn for other parts. There were many, many Marys, and many, many Josephs. The narrator reminded us that Jesus came into the world, just like us, and has promised to be in the midst of us. Jesus came so that all of us can be Joseph and Mary, participating in the act of bringing Christ into the world. All of us have a part in the gospel story, the Good News. We are those, the narrator said, who are bringing God's love into the world.

Truly, this pageant, like no other pageant before it, touched everyone who saw it. I share this story to remind us, at this stage of the church growth process, that it is a scary process to hand over responsibility and trust to new people, young people, even when they are previously known to us. I doubted my daughter, and doubted my community. Not because they were not good people, but because we were stepping out into uncharted territory and the script was unwritten. It is much, much, easier to complain about the old script and to stay with what we have done before because it is familiar. Like an old worn blanket that has lived past its usefulness, we still wrap ourselves in the old ways because they are safe to us. Growth demands that we move beyond safety and comfort. That move is hard for every human being.

As we move through this final chapter, remember that moving from safety and comfort to new ways of inclusion will present great anxiety for everyone. Even those folks who have made loud noise about wanting to grow and change will, at some point, have difficulty with the growth that they are inviting. This most transforming step will require that everyone be patient and tender with one another, and that the normal human anxiety responses are to be expected. Those responses are not judgments of individuals nor do they herald the failure of the effort to grow. They actually announce that growth has happened and is continuing to happen. Like the shepherds in the fields, remember to fear not. Those long ago shepherds were surrounded by beings that they did not understand, and they were frightened. They had every reason to be frightened. But the angels told them not to fear. "For behold, unto you is born this day in the City of David, a Savior, which is Christ the Lord."

There is much to fear at this point, but there is also much to be gained. The work of becoming a new people of God and finding new names for home can be scary. Fear not, for others have come this way and have been afraid, too. The shepherds found that as they stepped out in faith, God provided the necessary courage. Here are ten things to consider as you move through this next phase of the work of growing a congregation. They may seem like very simple things to remember, but many churches lose sight of their goals because they have lost their energy, their hope, or their capacity to see a positive future. These simple things will help everyone get through the most challenging situations.

1. **Take small steps.** If any task seems too large for one person, break up the work into smaller pieces and share them with others.

2. **Take time to pray.** Every day, every hour, alone or with a group—God is listening.

3. **Share food whenever possible.** Remember that the disciples knew Jesus in the breaking of the bread. Our honest selves are shared as we share food together.

4. **Keep breathing.** Whenever anxiety overtakes, focus on the most normal and life-giving things—like breathing.

5. **Tell stories.** Stories from our lives are rich with insight and meaning. We can often find God's at work in the midst of our lives, as we tell stories to one another.

6. **Ask for help.** No one person knows everything. That's why we live in communities. When we practice asking for help, others will know that their expertise (or lack of it) is welcome in your midst.

7. **Laugh a lot.** Everything in life is easier when we laugh. Some people think they have to be serious in church. If you don't take yourself or your tasks too seriously, even the difficult tasks will be "do-able."

8. **Take only the steps you need to take, make only the decisions you need to make for this part of your growth process.** Don't look too far down the road.

9. **No one should sit alone at gatherings, including you as leader.** When someone sits by us, we are reminded we are not alone. The message most of us need to see, hear, and feel is that we are not alone.

10. **Call each other and thank each other regularly.** Gratitude and connection are the signs of a lively relationship. When we do something routine and are thanked for it, we are reminded that what we take for granted might be a blessing to another. When we reach out and talk with others, we can be blessed and renewed in a very simple act of great love.

A New People of God

Then I saw a new heaven and a new earth . . . And I heard aloud voice from the throne saying, "See the home of God is among mortals. God will dwell with them as their God; they will be God's people, and God will be with them." (Revelation 21:1, 4)

In the book of Revelation, we hear this promise of God's dwelling being with mortals, with human beings, people like you and me. In ancient times, the thought of God dwelling with the regular folks was considered absurd and beyond consideration. In Jesus, we find that God comes to us in the form of a child, dwelling among us, understanding and living the life of our joys and our suffering. Too often this passage in Revelation is read at funerals, as if it foretells only what heaven or the afterlife might be like. Those who have captured Revelation for their sci-fi version of the rapture, where non-believers are left to rot on earth while believers are instantaneously drawn into heaven, also miss the real implications of the gift of Jesus. He came, in the humblest of situations, to stressed and challenged people, in the midst of a political crisis, and lived just as we do. He came, not to remove us from this world, but to take on the world and make us new in him. We are, by the gift of God in Jesus, a new people, real people, and God has promised to be with us.

We might be old and physically challenged, our community might be broken because of tragedy, we might be people with few financial resources, but God is in the midst of us. God is in this mess with us and has been every hour of every day. For me, that is where this new people of God can start as we work to grow our community of faith. We can celebrate that God is in our midst, no matter how limited, challenged, and compromised we might feel.

This is to say clearly that to be a New People of God, is not something we do, but is something that we have been given. We are a new people of God by virtue of Christ's activity and presence on this earth. We have all received this as a gift of God. Those who have been in your church forever have the same gift as those who have just arrived. Those who have fallen away, or who have quarreled with us, or who do not like the way we are changing—all of them have the same gift. The people of God are us, in the process of becoming made new by God's grace, and as we grow together in community. So this chapter is really about growing into something we already have, and opening up fully the amazing gift we have already been given.

Recently I had the great blessing of participating in a very historic ordination. I truly believe that when a community has raised up a leader from among their midst, a new chapter in their lives begins. Together, they become a new people of God. Some ordinations may change their community only slightly, but many can have a ripple effect that transforms everyone. Now, for a bishop, ordinations, especially in June and December, are common occurrences, as familiar as weddings to a parish priest. I am reluctant to admit it, but it is often hard, years later, to remember a specific ordination among many, unless something unusual or comical occurred. This is a day I will never forget, and I hope that the Episcopal Church will remember it always. This priestly ordination was neither comical, nor unusual in that it happened in December and was scheduled on a Sunday morning in a small, rural parish among the people that had raised up this leader for ordination. What was so memorable and historical about this ordination was that after four hundred years, the Episcopal Church finally ordained an Indigenous person from Virginia. In 1607, when the Church of England celebrated its first Eucharist on these shores, and several years later, with the conversion of Chanco and Pocahontas (Mataoka), our church has prided itself on the mission to Native American people. Our nation's history and our real survival, especially during the year 2007 with the 400th anniversary of the historic landing at Jamestown, rests on the shoulders and lives of the people who first welcomed the church to these shores. And yet, despite great mission and faithfulness in some places, our church had all but ignored the people who welcomed, fed, and clothed us in our early days. In recent history, that has all changed, due to the efforts of some tenacious men and women, and the bishops and priests who encouraged them and stuck with them.

The Monacan people have lived for centuries in the mountains of southwestern Virginia, and have clung to their culture and their faith despite mistreatment, first from settlers and trappers, and then from federal, state, and local governments. They were denied a secondary education by the state until the late twentieth century, along with the other seven tribes in Virginia. Their small community never lost hope and with generosity and compassion welcomed the missionaries who came to share the gospel and teach in their small school. Despite the fact that they were treated like second-class citizens throughout much of their history since 1607, they never lost hope and remained faithful.

On a brisk, chilly December morning with sunlight surrounding them and the brilliant gold and reds of late fall leaves, folks gathered outside a small white clapboard chapel, St. Paul's, nestled in the mountains, where Phyllis Hicks was to be made a priest in Christ's church. Many people, living and dead, who had waited expectantly, prayerfully, and anxiously over generations, seemed to be gathered around on this first Sunday in Advent, in this tiny love-filled, overflowing church. Phyllis knelt quietly among the gathered clergy and bishops, and the whole community rejoiced as Bishop Neff Powell's hands were laid on her head, then other clergy laid hands on her and leaned in, as the prayer was said; and she stood, receiving the fulfillment of God's promise for herself and her people. This humble church, filled with joyous music, became as movingly beautiful as a great cathedral; many were moved to tears. In her willingness to serve her people, and in her people's diligence and faithfulness, was an example of the fulfillment God's promise of inspiration and empowerment for all people.

Like many others who God calls to leadership, Phyllis sometimes carefully, sometimes even reluctantly responded to this call. She did not want to be "in charge," but she has a love in her heart for her people. The Rev. B. Lloyd, who has been urging her on for sixteen years, along with Bishop Frank N. Powell and retired Bishop Heath Light, can attest to her humility and gentle, constant devotion to her people. This community that once felt it had little future, now brims with the expectation of a bright future. Because Phyllis and others took on the story of her people, their real-life needs and dreams, a community, a diocese, and a whole church changed for the better. We can see God's promises unfolding before our eyes in their lives and their common work. Their willingness to take seriously their story and God's story promises to grow and enliven a whole broad spectrum of people, folks who would never before have believed that a small, rural, isolated community might become a beacon of light and Christ's promises for many.

Over the past months, a group of people in your church community has been meeting, reading the scriptures, listening to each other's stories, and identifying the gifts of individuals and your community. You have been mentoring and companioning others and you have been cared for and taught in return. You will also have witnessed a great many challenges as you have worked to invite others into you church community, desiring to grow both your church and the mission of your community. If you have approached this venture with even the smallest bit of investment of time and human capital, you will have collected a vast amount of information. You will also have witnessed and shared in cultural experiences, educational opportunities, and special events that have really changed the nature and daily life of your church family. In this season, you are invited to examine the gifts you have been given—those you have discovered hidden in plain sight, and all the insights you have gained in your sharing and work with others. What may well have emerged is an articulate vision of who God is calling you to be as a community. You have made a huge collage, with images from all around you, and now you have the opportunity to respond to God's gift of Christ in your midst.

The task for this season, whether you undertake it during Advent or some other time of the church year, is to gather up all of the information, impressions, expressions, and relationships that have become visible over the past months and determine together if there is any common theme or idea that stands out. This might be called a "collage exercise," where you put the fractured pieces of your lives together, holding them in tension with all the data that you have gathered. Sometimes, the best way to do this is to gather a great group of people in one room and put all of the collected images in one place. People can take time to look over photos, charts, and other information. Then you might want to ask yourselves the following series of very simple questions. Remember, there are no right or wrong answers here; there are just those directions and insights that God has revealed as you did this work together in community.

Together, you will be seeking the new people of God that you are becoming; you will be listening to angels, who are heralding a new life, a new season, a new direction for your community. Some people like to put these questions on a piece of paper for each person to fill out. Others recommend having a general discussion with everyone participating. At this point, you know that within your community there are people who do better in conversation and those who do best with pen and paper. You might offer both tools—discussion or writing or other approaches—as you determine how best to encourage the widest participation. Try to provide as many ways as possible for people to enter into this very important discussion. The work of growing a congregation is always most successful when a truly diverse group of people have input.

- Who is God calling us to be?

- What is God calling us to do?

- In what concrete ways do we see ourselves becoming a new people?

- How do we respond to God's call?

- What do we need to make this response?

- How can we tell others about God's call in our lives?

Some people in your community might not have a response to all the questions, but might have a good idea about one or two. Advent is a time of waiting, growing, and opening ourselves to God. These questions encourage those habits and activities of the season. These questions are meant to stimulate our creativity and our spirit, and to help the whole community to imagine themselves as a new people in God. This process is the work of weaving our stories into the stories of the living God, and of intertwining our lives with one another and the mission of God.

Some years ago, I was preaching in a small parish during the fall. It was the last Sunday before Advent, and right before Thanksgiving. The practice in the parish was to have a simple sermon since the children were in church for the whole service. In this parish, the children read the lessons and led the prayers for the church service at least every six weeks. I gathered the children around me for an informal children's sermon and talked with them about the coming of Jesus at Christmas. I asked them simple questions about how their families got ready for Christmas. We talked about the idea that during Advent we are waiting for the coming of Jesus. And they told me that Jesus came into the world as a little baby. It struck me that they were good children and very respectful—to this point. I then asked them how people they knew got ready for the coming of a baby; asked them how people make room for a new life in their family. They talked about sharing rooms, setting up a nursery, and babies crying at night. Then one little girl chimed in, "You have to have a shower!" She went on to ask if we could have a shower for the baby Jesus.

While the adults were snickering and lapping up this cute moment, I asked the children what might we want to bring to a shower for baby Jesus? One child said, "diapers," another "bottles," and they talked about car seats, strollers, and other items they could name. For a moment, I thought we were really getting off track. Then one of the children said, "Jesus was a poor child, he was born in a stable! He didn't have that stuff!" I reminded everyone that the kid had made a good point: that Jesus came into the world poor, and without much and far away from his family's home. And then that same little girl chimed in, saying that we could have a baby shower for baby Jesus and take all the things we collected to poor families. Well, there we were, on a Sunday morning, in the middle of the service, with a prophet in our midst. And so that's just what we did. The outreach folks got together and identified a women's shelter that took mothers with infants. They put out the word across the parish. We collected all sorts of baby items, and had people bring them during Advent.

At the end of our Christmas pageant, all of the children went to the back of the sanctuary (in costume) and brought up all the gifts that had been collected for baby Jesus and piled them on the floor of the crèche. They pushed strollers full of diapers, and carried baskets full of bottles, formula, and bibs. Several small children pushed car seats up to the front of the sanctuary, and one small child handed the baby Jesus a little stuffed animal. In that moment, our story and our community became entwined with the story of Jesus. The willingness of children to imagine God in our midst pushed us all to reach out to others, seeking the presence of the living God in the real everyday life of the smallest and most vulnerable in our midst. It took our vulnerable ones to break open our hearts and to point us to the star. The gift of the Christ child at Christmas was our story; we were part of the great drama of God's love being spread across our community.

This conversion and movement of an entire community to mission was begun by an innocent discussion with children. By taking seriously their input, and by creating space and time to listen, a community was able to respond to the question about what God was calling them to do. Not a forever or permanent task, but an answer to, "Lord, what should we be doing now?" By drawing the community together and understanding your shared gifts and challenges, a church community can become a new people of God. A new people of God, forged with and by the most vulnerable and tentative, as well as with and by the most permanent members of your congregation. If we are to be Christ's people in the world, we will have to equip one another, listen to others, and respond to the needs around us.

When you have met together and found some common themes or directions, make sure that everyone who comes through your doors knows what these might be. You are becoming a new people of God, but transitions are always difficult. Make sure that everyone has something that reminds them of what God is calling you to do, and make sure that they are invited to respond to that call. You may have decided, for example, that you have a special call to serve children in your community. Someone with a bit of creativity could create a logo on the computer and have it printed as an insert to the bulletin, with pictures and ideas for how individuals and families can participate in this mission.

Strangers No More

The disciples said, "Stay with us, because it is almost evening and the day is now nearly over." So he went to stay with them. When he was at table with them, he took bread, blessed and broke it, and gave it to them. Then their eyes were opened and they recognized him. (Luke 24:29–31)

The disciples were walking the seven miles from Jerusalem to Emmaus. They had been through great tragedy, they had watched Jesus die a horrible death, and they were skeptical about the story of the women who reported finding Jesus alive at the tomb. They had worked so hard, and believed so much, and now they were faced with going forward completely alone, completely diminished. They encountered a stranger on the road, who took up with them, talking and walking alongside them. We all know now that in the end, Jesus came and ate with them, and they recognized him. A horrible, unbearable moment in their lives was turned around. And it was the stranger who turned their lives around. It is ironic and yet true, that it is when we open ourselves to strangers, when we welcome the one who is bothering us, walking with us, the one who is wondering and asking—it is exactly when we are on the road, dusty and dirty, that we find Jesus in our midst.

All of us came to a community as strangers. All of us come to a community to be welcomed as a friend, a family member, or at least an invited guest. All too often in the life of our church, we keep our distance from newcomers, as if they will remind us that we were once strangers here and once needed the help of others to know how to survive in this place.

Truth be told, we often don't risk welcoming others because we hate to admit our own vulnerability, our own closeness to the edge. Jesus' disciples were on the edge, and wondered what to do with a strange character late at night. They welcomed him in and fed him. Simple acts are those in which God's true love for the world is revealed. When a church community is willing to welcome people in and feed them, willing to respond to the needs of the strangers in their midst, then the distance between stranger and member is no more. When we honor the bodily and spiritual needs of those who pass by, we honor the needs of Christ in this world. And Christ is revealed to us anew, as he was revealed to the disciples in that dark roadhouse meal, so many years ago.

As we face this season of Advent as a church community committed to growth, we are being called to make the stranger at home among us. For some communities, that might mean welcoming back those who have left over disputes and making a place for them. In other communities, folk might feel separated out because of age (too young, too old), or because they feel they have no place, no gift to bring to the community. This is the season and the time in the process of growth to open the gates, to let down the barriers, and to find every possible way to announce that there are no more strangers at the table with Christ.

One of the simplest ways to open the doors of our hearts and to incorporate strangers in our midst (remembering that strangers can refer to *all of us*) is to begin small groups who meet for a meal and/or for prayer. Many individuals find it difficult to enter into the larger community on Sunday morning, but are much more comfortable if they are included in a simple gathering at someone's home. Some of the most successful groups consist of no more than ten people, meeting on a regular basis (weekly or twice a month), who take time to listen to one another and include each other in their prayers. Churches that are seeing growth, report that when at least half of the adults in their community are involved in some sort of small group, whether for prayer, fellowship, or a combination of both, find that their community is growing at a tremendous rate. They also report that their church communities are more diverse if they are willing to share simple fellowship in small groups.

As an Advent discipline, beginning small groups would allow new folks to be incorporated into the life of a parish, over the four weeks of the season, seeking some commonality among the more established in your church community. The folks who engage in these small groups might want to agree to some simple rules, like keeping the group meeting time to two hours or under, and to not judging, criticizing, or acting as therapists to one another. Like Jesus walking with the disciples, these small group members would be sharing their reactions to events in their lives, and then sharing a meal together. The desired spiritual transformation, the growth in a community, and the presence of the living Christ in our lives comes when we engage in walking this journey of faith with others. Throughout the gospels, prayer and a simple shared meal are the most normal and common ways Jesus shared himself and the Good News of God's love present in this world. These two things are the way we move from stranger to friend in the family of God and our local communities of faith. It remains the way we open our hearts to God and one another.

In the previous chapter, I suggested that having mentors and companions was one way to build relationships across differences, whether generational or cultural. If you have taken up this idea, it might be well to involve those people who have had some success with their mentoring and companioning to act as hosts for a prayer or fellowship group. Always go with the skills and gifts that you have among you. Also, remember that for some individuals, there may be barriers to participating in a small group. Some might not have transportation, another might have a difficult work schedule, and yet another may not drive at night. Others may be shut in and unable to travel while others might have a language or cultural barrier that the leadership of the church community may not readily know about. Folks with children may have childcare needs. Many churches, which fail to grow when they have the potential, often overlook the critical needs of parents with young children.

For folks to participate in small groups, or in any other roles in the church community, a constant effort must be made to find ways to open doors, invite others, and care for their needs, so that they can grow into a relationship with the church family. Most people want to be more involved and often shy away because they don't know how to enter in light of their specific circumstances. It is important to make sure that there is an individual, or better yet, a team of folks who could respond to those concerns without drawing attention to the individual concerned.

Once Christmas has come, these groups might continue, being a common ground where those who were once new would have an expanded "family" with which to share their holidays. In the New Year, the entire parish does not have to make an ongoing commitment to small groups, but can assess whether these groups have provided a level of inclusion for newcomers and more established members alike. There might be folks who have found a particular group too critical or confining, or there may be personalities who should not be committed long term to the same group. All of the concerns that might arise will be overshadowed by the reality that strangers have been included in the life of the community in a way that many have never experienced before. The interpersonal conflicts that might arise from folks spending time together sharing food and prayer will definitely be overshadowed by the deepening of relationships and commitment between people and in the midst of the community. What a gift to give others at Christmas—a community with an open heart, people with their doors open to strangers, and tables and hearts overflowing with God's bounty and presence.

Renaming Home

When Jesus came into the district of Caesarea Philippi, he asked his disciples, "Who do people say that the Son of Man is?" And they said, "Some say John the Baptist, but other Elijah, and still some others Jeremiah or one of the prophets." He said to them, "But who do you say that I am?" Simon Peter answered, "You are the Messiah, the Son of the living God." And Jesus answered him, "Blessed are you, Simon, son of Jonah! For flesh and blood have not revealed this to you, but my Father in heaven. And I tell you, you are Peter, and on this rock I will build my church, and the gates of Hades will not prevail against it. I will give you the keys of the kingdom of heaven, and whatsoever you bind on earth will be bound in heaven, and whatever you loose on earth will be loosed in heaven." (Matthew 16:13–19)

In many ancient traditions, when someone's life has changed, he or she often gets a change of name. We see this in the gospel of Matthew and through out the gospels, where we find Jesus telling Simon, in one way or another, that his name was to be Peter, or Cephas, translated as "rock." Peter is the central character of the founding of the Christian Church and Jesus refers to building on this rock, this Peter.

In Native American traditions, we also have the custom of renaming people when they have done something heroic, or if their life has changed drastically. This custom posed (and continues to pose) great problems for census takers and the Indian agents responsible for tribal roles. The same man or woman might appear with several names, all of which they answer to, and many that other people associate with them. Adding to this is the complicated problem of naming and renaming, which happens in family groups. Among tribal people, it is not uncommon to have several names, one or more of which is used only within the confines of a family unit. David Pendelton Oakerhater, the great Cheyenne warrior and the first American Indian on the calendar of the Episcopal Church, took David Pendelton Oakerhater as his full Christian name, but was also called Making Medicine, along with several other names. Many traditions and groups have very specific cultural rules and some have taboos about how names are given, and by whom. Names were very important to Jesus, just as names have significant power and authority to many of our tribal peoples and to other racial and ethnic groups.

With all the work that your church community has taken on to grow your capacities, broaden your mission, uncover the many gifts in your community, and in making the church a place of sanctuary and healing, it is time to find a new name. It is time for a new name because you are no longer what you once were as a church community and your heartfelt desire is to incorporate the newer people in your midst. It is time for a new name that declares what you are becoming together, and which can make room for those who will join the community after a new name is declared. It is time to make known the movement of God in the lives of the people. As Mary could not hide forever that she was with child and would have to face the wrath and ridicule of her community, so too, your growth has changed your appearance to many outside of your parish family. For some, both inside and outside, this reality may be uncomfortable, embarrassing, and/or mystifying. A new name will help others understand what has transpired and continues to transpire in your community, along with declaring for yourselves that you are different.

Before you get upset and are tempted to slam this book shut, I am not asking you to shed the beloved name of your church. Your parish or mission was founded and named either after a patron saint like Peter, Paul, or Anne, or after a theological concept like Grace, the Holy Trinity, the Incarnation, the Holy Spirit, or the Holy Comforter. Or you might have been named after Christ himself. It would be foolish to destroy the long history of commitment to the place and the people who have lived in faith, worshipped within these walls, and seen the movement of God in their lives and in their times. Rather, this new name would augment the church's present name, adding a new and deeper identity declared for all to see and understand. This new name would be added to the letterhead, stationery, and maybe even grace a banner, so that the whole faith community could begin to embrace their new identity.

Practically, when coming up with a new name, it is best to keep it short and precise. You are adding to a church name. Many outsiders and newcomers to your church community might even be confused over your present name. Many folks probably don't correctly identify your congregation as they mishear and mispronounce the denomination in which I serve, the Episcopal Church. Confusion abounds, so I suggest that you try to be as clear as possible about who you are and where you stand. People don't need "clever" when they are seeking a church community; they need to hear and see a clear invitation, and feel a tangible, visceral sense of welcome. Whatever you do in this renaming process, be careful not to confuse people by fancy words and catchy phrases. Churches cannot grow when people stand outside and say, "Huh?"

Devising a new name during this season of Advent, or whenever you chose to use this chapter, should be a joyful process in which everyone in your community may participate. This process might fall quickly on the heels of the work that was done earlier in the chapter entitled a New People of God. You have already announced to folks the common themes and mission of your church community. You have looked over all of the information you have collected over the months and found ways to express your identity—who you are and who God is calling you to be. The next step is to state simply what is already going on in your lives. Here are some examples of new church names:

St. Peter's Church—A Praying Community

St. Anne's—Singing God's Praises

St. Thomas's—Building a Home for All

St. Martha's—Feeding Everyone

St. Paul's—We Need You!

Recently, I have been fascinated by a sign that I pass as I drive to church on Sunday mornings. This sign is on the awning that covers the entrance to a downtown urban church in a community that has faced many financial hardships, racial unrest, and political shakeups. The church is Pentecostal and declares, "Where the blood line erases the color line!" It took me several times of driving by to fully take in what they were saying, or at least what I believe they are saying. They are saying that in the blood of Jesus, there is no difference due to race. This is a bold statement to make, especially in a community that has historically been very divided by race, and one that continues to struggle with the issues of poverty and inadequate and unequal access to social services. I can't help but wonder how the people of this church decided to make this their statement to the world. They have touched a nerve in me, and I hope that sometime soon, I can go and ask them about it.

Remember that this renaming process is very much a celebration of the gifts you have uncovered in your midst. It is a celebration of growth, excitement, and possibility. This new naming process is not meant to solidify your theology or make the community more unilateral; rather, your new name is a way of inviting the best of who you are to open up to the best of those who are seeking a community, a home, a group of people who will journey along with you; and you will hear their stories, welcome their gifts, and make their stories part of the life of the whole community.

This is a spiritually charged moment in the life of your local church. It can challenge the more traditional, solidly grounded identity and challenge your community to identify how it has changed. It can chafe and irritate people to even think that their beloved church community will continue to change. Be aware that you are treading on sensitive ground. Many folks come to church hoping to find a place that, in the midst of a confusing and rapidly changing world, a parish community that will be a constant for them, and a place where they may never have to deal with change. Reminding each other that we are constantly in a state of change, both individually and corporately, while helpful to some, might not be helpful to others. Remember to be clear, that as you grow and change in order to welcome others, the story of the original community and their gifts will not be lost in the midst of those who come to join you. In fact, their stories and their gifts will be the rich, solid ground that supports and helps others to flourish. It is their story, their gifts, and their commitment that has made possible the growth, the welcome of others, and the continuing positive transformation of your church family.

I want to share another story with you at this point. When my family and I lived in suburban Philadelphia and I was serving in a church nearby, we adopted a dog from the pound. This dog was a German Shepherd mix, sweet and energetic, and our three daughters named her Madeline (after the children's story)—since she was the youngest girl in line. Like most animals do, she quickly became an integral part of our family life, making messes and demanding attention like everyone else. When Madeline was with us for several years, she somehow got out of our yard and went missing. We immediately started driving through the neighborhood calling her name. After many hours had gone by, and darkness had settled in, we gave up for the night. Our girls were inconsolable. Weeping and howling went on, and didn't seem to abate as the days went by. We posted brilliantly colored signs throughout our neighborhood, and beyond, and offered a reward.

Several times we got phone calls from people who thought they might have seen her, but they said it could have been a small deer they saw—and she was running fast. Sounded like Madeline, but we never had any luck when we went to the location they described. Many weeks went by and we had really given up hope. Early one Sunday, about three in the morning, I woke up, disturbed by something. Our bedroom was on the third floor so I went downstairs to check on the children, who were all sound asleep. I tiptoed downstairs and couldn't really hear anything that would have woken me up. I checked the doors and then opened the driveway side door and looked outside. In ran Madeline, skinny and weak, with no bark left. She had crawled up onto the hood of our van and was whimpering, best I could figure. The house erupted to my screams and cries and my husband and our daughters came tumbling down the stairs. None of us slept anymore that night.

I share this story with you to remind you that if a lost mutt can find her way home, and if a very sleepy adult can somehow hear the whimpering of an exhausted animal, how much more so does God listen to and never fail to look for us. And if God is capable of welcoming us in the middle of the night, when all hope is gone, can we not give a small measure of that welcome home to people who are desperately seeking God through and in our communities. If we can become a beacon of hope, we can be a way home to God for many.

You might try to remind the regulars in your congregation that their solid gifts, their constancy, will be honored for the blessing and sturdy foundation that an ever-living church community needs for continued growth. And remember, that this season, whether you engage this chapter during Advent or another season, is holy ground. The immediate world around us all is changing. God is in the midst of you, and things that were predictable and steady, may seem less so now. Go carefully and thoughtfully with each other and all you welcome in your midst, for Christ came this way in the night, bringing peace to friends and strangers, to the fearful and the zealous, to the meek and arrogant. Growth, like all other outward signs in our common life, is a gift from God, and not something we can control.

Attention to Ritual

Sunday mornings will take on some new challenges during this chapter of the book, whether you attempt to do this during Advent, or another season of the church year. You are probably wondering how exactly I am proposing you move through the rites and rituals of the season as well as include the learning and insight that has taken place during the past few weeks. You might be asking one or more of the following questions. How do we design our worship in a way that reflects us as a new people of God? How do we worship God together as we seek to hear our new name on the lips of the people? How can we worship and welcome the stranger, visitor, and companion, and give their story a place in the midst of the other stories of our community? And how do we do this with a little over an hour on Sunday mornings? You might even be wondering what you have gotten yourself into and, considering the season of the year, think about delaying whole process while you try to get through the overwhelming demands of the season (particularly if this is Advent for you).

I want to reassure you that there is less need to focus on Sunday mornings with this process than you might have expected. This is a perfect time to provide people with ways to take their community and their stories home.

I want to suggest that for this season the simplest addition to your common worship service is the best. What you want to be doing on Sunday morning together is listening and sharing the great news of God in Jesus Christ. You want to focus on telling the story of God's promise of Jesus, the Savior of the world, who came into the world as a stranger, for strangers. This emphasis on Jesus Christ coming into the world as a stranger for strangers, and weaving the story of your people with the story of God's promise that we are all family in Christ—well, this might just be exactly enough for your time on Sundays. Jesus was born outside of the norms of the religious community of his day, and he was born to parents who were exiled, often finding themselves in strange circumstances. This story is something that everyone can relate to, can find their own circumstances in this incredible story.

One of the simple exercises that might be useful for this season is to develop a prayer that centers and collects your church community at this time and season. Years ago, I worked with a team of Native leaders in the Episcopal Church developing what would become the Indigenous Theological Training Institute. This was an effort to develop a community-based training for Native American leaders in the Episcopal Church. As part of this process, it was decided that to do this life-changing work, we would have to have a community prayer—something that bound us all together and which we could all use on a regular basis, in all the work and worship settings we encountered. Embedded in this prayer is not only recognition of the uniqueness of the community that we were developing, but the uniqueness of the people who were gathering to do this work. As Native Christians, it is a prayer that could also reflect the breadth of who we were, from diverse tribes and religious experiences. Since that time, over ten years ago, it has been used in a variety of gatherings, as well as in people's homes and in their daily devotions. Entitled "The Gathering Prayer," I share it here as an example of what a group can create that can be used for Sunday worship and in many other settings.

The Gathering Prayer

Creator, we give you thanks for all you are and all you
  bring to us for our visit within your creation.
In Jesus, you place the Gospel at the Center of this
  Sacred Circle through which all of creation is related.
  You show us the way to live a generous and
  compassionate life.
Give us your strength to live together with respect and
  commitment as we grow in your spirit, for you are God,
  now and forever. Amen.

This prayer, and other resources from the Native Ministries Office of the Episcopal Church can be found on line as part of the Episcopal Church's website. There are other liturgical resources available from the website as well.

I would also suggest that those who might be preaching make sure that they share stories of times when they felt far off from God, and how they were gathered in. Making the connection with people who are new to your community means saying out loud that once you did not feel that you were really a part of the community. Tell people how you finally did begin to become a part of the whole, part of the family. Any way you can reveal the nature of God in community, the commonality of being a stranger, and the reality of God's presence and love drawing us into communities of faith will support the work that is being done for inclusion and growth. Remember that community itself is a gift from God, a gift to be shared, and not something controlled or controllable. The more ways that these basic truths are said out loud and demonstrated in worship and fellowship, the more possible it is for people to draw near.

Stewardship

In Chapter Four I suggested that you might want to think of stewardship and your fund raising needs in the context of the abundance of gifts that you have discovered in community. You have done an enormous amount of work over the past months, learning from and listening to the folks around you. Together, you have discovered many gifts and challenges in your midst and have, by this point, begun to find ways to design your stewardship efforts with these discoveries in mind. I want to share one final story from my grandfather WalkingStick, which I hope reminds us all about our complete interdependence on one another and on God. We have resources and skills we have gained, but it is God who does the giving, and the greatest of these gifts often come in our darkest moments.

Grandfather told us this story.

The Cherokees had developed a type of field corn over the ages that would make or complete its growth, if we had good rain, in late June. There was always plenty of rain before that date, but drought usually set in late in June or early July for the rest of the summer. It was a short, fat ear of corn, about half as long as our present hybrid corn. It always made a crop. There was plenty of corn. There was an old stone mill run by a Cherokee on a creek about four miles from my grandfather's place. We would take our corn for cornmeal (to make cornbread) and our wheat for flour to this mill. The miller would grind it while one waited, and he would keep a third for his work. My grandfather WalkingStick once let me take a sack of corn (shelled, of course) to the mill. I was about ten years old. I could go by the wagon road, which was much longer, or I could take the path over the hills. I took the path, for I knew it, and I rode bareback. Grandfather placed the sack of grain astride the horse in front of me and saw to it that it was well balanced. I took off in high spirits, for I had taken another step toward useful adulthood and wished to do well. About halfway, up among the timbered hills, something caused my horse to shy, or dart sideways, possibly a chipmunk, snake, the bite of a horsefly, or simply a bad dream as this old horse acted as if he were asleep half the time. The sack of grain fell off. I tried every way I could think of to put it back up on the horse's back. It was too heavy for me. I squirmed and twisted and lifted all I could, until I finally gave out. I was so frustrated that I simply sat down on a rock and cried. I knew I would have to stay there until someone came along, for I couldn't leave the grain to the animals, but this was a seldom used trail and it might be a day or so until someone came along. I had given up life as hopeless and I was letting my grandfather down.

That old sleepy horse raised his droopy head and pointed his ears back down the trail. He had heard footsteps long before I did. Two Cherokees, a man and his wife, came into sight riding horses. My troubles were over. I said, "si-yo," hello, and blurted out my troubles. The man chuckled, jumped down, and lifted the sack and me onto the horse's back. I was so happy that I told the couple who I was, and to come visit us; and if they would come, I would go into the woods and shoot all the "so-lo-lee," squirrels, that they could eat. The squirrel bit I put in because to me there was no food on earth to compare with fried squirrel with gravy over hot cornbread. I was truly grateful. I went to the mill with the grain and had a quite grownup conversation with the miller about the condition of the crops, hunting and fishing, and the chance for rain soon. When I got home my grandfather told me I did well with the grain, but grandmother patted me all over and told me what a fine job I had done. I never did tell them I had cried.

Our stewardship efforts should always include the awareness that we are always precarious and challenged, even when we feel strong and capable. Any turn in the road can feel like the end of life as we know it. People in our congregations have families to provide for and are often more anxious and on edge about money than is ever articulated. Any way that we can share our abundance, any way we can help others hoist "the sack and me to the horse's back" will be an act of generosity that comes from the heart of God. As we ask one another to share our resources for the uplifting of others in need, I encourage you to also be aware, and watch for those in your midst who will need creative ways to offer their gifts. They may not have an abundance of dollars, but God has given them some gifts that can enrich the lives of the whole community. Listening to people's needs, while asking folks to contribute, will become an outward sign that your church community has the capacity to be generous in giving and receiving, making all people an essential part of the fabric and pulse of your parish.

Sanctuary

By the tender mercy of God, the dawn from on high will break upon us, to give light to those who sit in darkness and in the shadow of death, to guide our feet into the way of peace. (Luke 1:78–79)

These words are from Zechariah, the father of John the Baptist. He was silent throughout the time Elizabeth was carrying their son, and these word he speaks, as prophecy, filled with the Holy Spirit, declaring God's promise to use John to proclaim God's peace breaking into the world. We have read the whole story of John's ministry, and know that Zechariah's jubilant and hopeful prophecy was to be challenged by the violence of the world. John's life was hard and his death was harsh. Much of the world we live in and the people with whom we interact, experience life as harsh and violent. Most of the people who make up our church community, whether they have recently come or have been around for a long time, struggle with their overwhelming need to be part of something that gives them meaning and purpose. They desire a place where the violence of the world is challenged and they can know God as safe and secure, rather than violent, harsh, and judgmental. They want, as do we all, a place and a community in which they can glimpse that promise, that jubilation that Zechariah so clearly sees and knows as the presence of God.

This season, in this process of growth, is a time to find real ways to engage people in their struggle with violence in the world (and in each of us) and the promises that God has made to make us a community of healing, reconciliation, and peace. Sanctuary, in this sense, means harboring the notion that there is something other than greed and violence in our daily lives. It means engaging people in conversation and work that helps them find meaning and purpose in their lives and which helps them glimpse peace and joy breaking through their daily struggles. Your people, in dialog with each other, will decide how your church community will live out the ideal of sanctuary for themselves and others.

Our earlier conversations about sanctuary have focused on the real needs of human beings within the structures (buildings and relationships) of your church community. Safeguarding children, providing for accessibility and inclusion of the broadest range of folks is critical to the work of church growth. Giving people the opportunity to deal with issues of concern, either past or present, provides a healthy place in which folks can grow together in relationship with God. But sanctuary also must look outward to the broader community. Some people call this "outreach" and others call it "mission." Whatever you call it, encourage one another to find ways to joyfully express the gifts that you have been given. If you have found sanctuary in your church community, find ways to share that sanctuary with others. It may be providing a safe place for groups to congregate that others will not have. It might be reaching out to resettlement organizations, providing space for ESL (English as a second language), opening up your space for senior day care, or other ministries that provide welcome, hospitality, and sanctuary for those outside of your church family.

One church I know started a men's breakfast group because several men in their church were recently retired, and all of them had also been recently widowed. They opened the group up to any men in the community for breakfast fellowship and conversation. There was no religious aspect to their gathering, but rather they were providing a comfortable atmosphere for friendship. Over time, they got to know each other and found they had shared interests and abilities. Several got together and repaired a few second hand bikes that they had lying around, giving them to children in their neighborhood. After awhile, they realized that there were many families in their area who did not have the money for bicycles for their children. So they decided to start raising money so those children could have new bicycles for Christmas. The first year, they were so proud because they had raised enough to buy ten bicycles. Little by little this nonchalant project has become a year round effort and after several years, they are giving away over fifty bicycles at Christmas. Sanctuary can mean a cup of coffee and conversation and it can grow into a wonderful Christmas gift for another human being. It can grow from simple shelter and company to a means to transform the world around you.

EXERCISES

1. **Our Family Prayer Tree.** Display in a prominent place like the vestibule, entrance hall or parish hall, a totally bare Christmas tree that is strung with only a wide ribbon, wrap-

ping it from top to bottom and all the way around. Place a basket with scraps of shiny paper nearby, on which are written all the ministries of the parish and the names of people in the parish or congregation, and in your community. You will want to have brightly colored paper clips or some safety pins. During this Advent season, ask folks to chose a paper, sign their name to it, and pin the paper to the ribbon that decorates the Christmas tree. By doing this, they are committing to simply pray for someone or something daily during this season. They can chose as many as they want, and many people can pin up and be praying for the same things. Have plenty of blanks so that people can add their own prayers to the tree. Folks who are meeting in prayer groups can also pin up the prayers that they are raising during the season. Make sure someone takes a picture of the tree once the season is over, so that people can be reminded of the prayers that were said.

2. **Prayer blankets and shawls.** Many churches have a ministry of "prayer shawls," where people who knit get together and pray while they are knitting. The completed shawls are then given to people who have recently suffered loss, illness, or some other challenge in their lives. Other churches have committed to making or purchasing blankets or sleeping bags and have tied them with ribbons with prayers attached to them. These blankets and sleeping bags are then given to homeless shelters, women's shelters, and other social services that care for those who are without shelter and comfort. Some church communities commit to wrapping up baby items this way, so that new mothers in challenging circumstances might know of their prayers. You might ask a cross section of folks to write simple prayers that could be reproduced and tied onto the ribbons. Young people, children, and newcomers might also be asked to design a picture or graphic of your community that could be reproduced along with the prayers.

Works Cited

Berg, Bruce L. *Qualitative Research Methods for the Social Sciences* (3rd ed.). Needham Heights, MA: Allyn and Bacon, 1998.

Gardner, Howard. *Leading Minds.* New York: HarperCollins, 1995.

Patton, Michael Quinn. *Qualitative Evaluation and Research Methods* (2nd ed.). Newbury Park, CA: Sage Publications, 1990.

Ryan, P. M. *Dictionary of Modern Maori.* Auckland, NZ: Heinemann, 1994.

CPSIA information can be obtained
at www.ICGtesting.com
Printed in the USA
LVHW090253220120
644357LV00001B/7